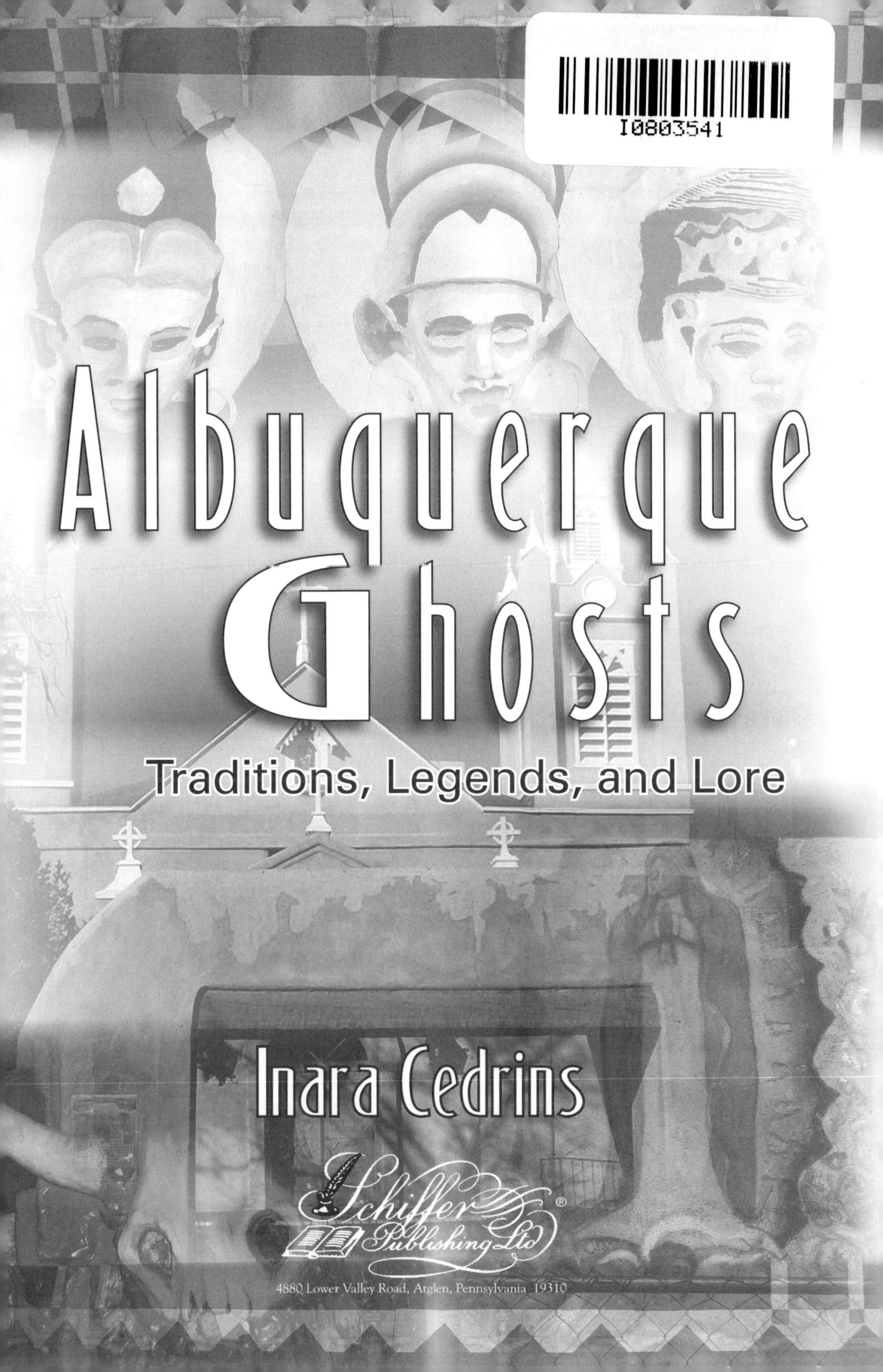

Albuquerque Ghosts

Traditions, Legends, and Lore

Inara Cedrins

Schiffer Publishing Ltd®
4880 Lower Valley Road, Atglen, Pennsylvania 19310

Schiffer Books are available at special discounts for bulk purchases for sales promotions or premiums. Special editions, including personalized covers, corporate imprints, and excerpts can be created in large quantities for special needs. For more information contact the publisher:

Published by Schiffer Publishing Ltd.
4880 Lower Valley Road
Atglen, PA 19310
Phone: (610) 593-1777; Fax: (610) 593-2002
E-mail: Info@schifferbooks.com

For the largest selection of fine reference books on this and related subjects, please visit our web site at **www.schifferbooks.com**
We are always looking for people to write books on new and related subjects.
If you have an idea for a book please contact us at the above address.

This book may be purchased from the publisher.
Include $5.00 for shipping.
Please try your bookstore first.
You may write for a free catalog.

In Europe, Schiffer books are distributed by
Bushwood Books
6 Marksbury Ave.
Kew Gardens
Surrey TW9 4JF England
Phone: 44 (0) 20 8392-8585; Fax: 44 (0) 20 8392-9876
E-mail: info@bushwoodbooks.co.uk
Website: www.bushwoodbooks.co.uk
Free postage in the U.K., Europe; air mail at cost.

Library of Congress Control Number: 2008942800

Designed by Mark David Bowyer
Type set in Binner / Zurich BT

ISBN: 978-0-7643-3220-3
Printed in the United States of America

Contents

Introduction

Land of the Sacred and the Spiritual

Ghosts are history. They remain from prehistoric legends; come from the native stories of Mexico; were brought as myths by the Spanish and adapted to a new land. Those who died in times of violence remain in spirit, along with those who succeeded in trade, built and ruled mansions in New Mexico's famous golden light that their spirit perhaps does not want to cease enjoying.

New Mexico is unique in having rich Native American and Hispanic culture. Petroglyphs were carved into the lava rocks of West Mesa, a seventeen-mile-long table of land west of the Rio Grande in Albuquerque, by Native Americans 2,000 to 3,000 years ago; when sections became part of the Atrisco Land Grant after 1692, presented to certain colonists by the Spanish crown, they also left marks in the form of Christian crosses and cattle brands. Explorers of the 1800s chiseled their names and dates into the boulders.

The migrating spirit of the divine continues to manifest itself in the form of various religions and sects; as recently as 1992, Santa Fe and Albuquerque were cluster sites for Tibetan refugees. From cathedral to morada, synagogue to mosque, ashram to monastery, and stupa to retreat center, New Mexico hosts many houses of the holy – their beautiful ornamentation illustrating the beliefs and testifying to the commitment of its members and their belief in the spiritual. Many towns that flourished due to a specific function in the frontier past are now abandoned, and low humidity has preserved many of the buildings intact as "ghost towns."

Hispanic roots are highlighted at the National Hispanic Cultural Center and Coronado Monument, and there are Native American crafts festivals and feast days; some ceremonies and rituals are open to the public, some remain private. Acoma Pueblo, 370 feet above the desert floor and called "Sky City," is one of the oldest continuously occupied sites in North America. The state's highlights include legendary Route 66 that ran through eight states as a federal highway; ties to the past when the state was part of Mexico; and the folklore of cowboys and gunslingers of the West.

> "I think New Mexico was the greatest experience from the outside world that I have ever had."
>
> – D.H. Lawrence

Prehistoric Legends

Prehistoric humans, who camped in the Estancia Basin millennia ago, are called the Clovis people today, after the New Mexico town where their artifacts were first discovered. They were followed by the Folsom culture, when, as mammoths disappeared, tools were developed to hunt bison. And then Lake Estancia also disappeared, leaving low-lying "salines" that became salt ponds during the rainy season. Adapting, people roved the land for food. When they learned to plant corn, they settled; beans and squash were also grown. In 5 or 6 A.D., pottery began to be produced, so that cooking techniques could be developed, water collected, and storage provided.

In the Salinas Valley, two ancient southwestern cultures, the Mogollon and Anasazi, overlapped. As they developed, better agricultural techniques were brought in from Mexico, and Tompiro and Tiwa speaking people migrated from the Rio Grande, expanding settlements. By the tenth century, Mogollon villages flourished.

The first structures were pithouses, some entered through a doorway, those with firmer superstructure from a ladder through the roof; later there were above-ground *jacales* of adobe-plastered walls. The language pattern was set, with those living near present-day Albuquerque near the Rio Grande Valley speaking Tiwa.

A more advanced civilization two centuries later, centered on the Colorado Plateau, was that of the Anasazi, introduced through the

Cibola (Zuni) district and the Rio Grande pueblos, assimilating the Mogollon. The Anansazi built contiguous stone-and-adobe structures that formed the earliest stages of the pueblo society, also preserving the pithouses, probably for warmth in winter. Hunters and gatherers in about 2000 B.C., they are now regarded as the ancestors of all Puebloan people, by 1100 A.D. constructing intricate dwellings such as the 800-room Pueblo Bonito at Chaco Canyon. Most Anasazi sites in New Mexico were "Chaco outliers," as it was probably the religious or administrative capital. The Salinas Valley became a major trade center and one of the most populated parts of the pueblo world, with approximately 10,000 inhabitants by the seventeenth century.

Brush-and-mud *jacales* had evolved into large stone complexes. Doors were difficult to make and operate, also forming a weak spot that was difficult to defend; ceiling hatchways were easier to make and defend. The pithouse form became the kiva, an underground ceremonial chamber in the Anasazi culture. Sometimes the walls were painted with elaborate designs. Dances were meant to keep the universe in order, reverse the change in day's length, or bring rain. Stories, legends, and information were passed on in the kivas. The secular was not separate from the sacred: life depended on planting, hunting, and prayer.

Maize, pinon nuts, beans, squash, salt, and cotton goods were traded for dried buffalo meat, hides, flints, and shells. The inhabitants also raised turkeys, and hunted rabbits, deer, antelope, and bison. Fine black-on-white pottery was made, there was weaving and basket making.

Though at their height in about 1300, the Anasazi disappeared, and the nomadic Navajo migrated to the area, settling in the Rio Grande area, where Coronado's expedition found them in 1540 and irrevocably altered their lifestyle. It is thought that the Western Apache, nomadic hunters and gatherers who spoke a language of the Athapaskan stock, probably migrated south from northern Canada to the plains of Texas and New Mexico in the 1400s and 1500s, at about the same time that the pueblos were moving east and resettling mainly in the Rio Grande valley. They ranged from Texas to central Arizona, from far south in Mexico to the Peaks of Colorado.

Both movements were still going on when the Spanish colonizers arrived from the south, finding four groups of nomadic Indians. The Navajos and Gila Apaches lived west of the Rio Grande, Jicarilla Apaches and Mescaleros inhabited mountains and plains to the east. There were possibly more than 100 pueblos located along the Rio Grande Valley, from northern Taos Pueblo to southern Isleta Pueblo: today there are 19 pueblos in New Mexico, each sovereign, sharing a common prehistory and culture. While the Spanish brought in Catholicism, the traditional religions have also been preserved; both are observed in the pueblos, for cultural and spiritual reasons, coexisting in a process called compartmentalization.

At **Petroglyph National Monument**, volcanic eruptions occurring about 130,000 years ago created what is called "reverse topography," flowing down arroyos, forming peninsulas, and circling hills that then eroded to form canyons. Boulders that broke away from the basalt caprock bore a thin patina of dark desert varnish, and people discovered that they could chip into the surface to expose lighter-colored rock beneath and make drawings. The land was set aside in 1990 to protect and preserve the more than 25,000 petroglyphs that can still be viewed in their natural context, and is managed by the National Park Service in cooperation with the City of Albuquerque Open Space Division.

Petroglyphs

Petroglyphs

These are cultural images that bear deep significance for contemporary pueblos Indians and other native peoples. The relative age of the petroglyphs has been estimated through comparison with prehistoric pottery designs or wall paintings, the darkness of the image, its style or content. Perhaps ninety percent were created using the Rio Grande style, developed around 1300 A.D. when the local population increased rapidly, and villages were constructed along the river and in the foothills of the Sandia Mountains. Images include masks and masked figures, human hands and feet, and animals including mountain lions, birds, serpents, reptiles, and insects – geometric designs, spirals, and four-pointed stars.

Kokopelli, often called the "humpbacked flute player," appears in many forms, possibly spanning a wider area than any other single representational rock-art figure. It is suggested that the figure, which turns up not only across the Southwest and northern Mexico, but also in southern Mexico and Central America, originated in Peru more than 1000 years ago. Identifiable by an arched back and clarinet-like flute, Kokopelli is manifested in Southwestern rock art also as a kilt- and sash-clad human, a humpbacked rabbit, a mountain sheep or a locust. A charismatic figure, he seems able to impregnate women, lead migration, choreograph ceremonial dance, and bring hunting and farming success. Pivotal in ancient rituals, he may be dancing, sitting, lying or walking.

Representations and mythology of a rabbit on the moon are found in the art of ancient China and in Pre-Columbian Mexico (the super-nova of 1054 A.D. was recorded by both Chinese and Anasazi astronomers). Arriving in the Southwest, it took on the features of the native Blacktail Jackrabbit, appearing both on rock art and ceramics. Also it is Chinese tradition to hang small bells at the door so that they ring when someone enters; it is also thought that ghosts hate the sound of ringing bells and flee. Wind chimes provide like protection. There is some evidence that the ringing of church bells before service was intended to frighten away evil spirits so that worshippers could make it to the church unharmed.

Kokopelli figures dance on the wall behind a furniture store on Broadway, Albuquerque.

The **Zia sun**, symbol of the state of New Mexico, comes from Zia Pueblo, where ancestors of the inhabitants are thought to have come from Chaco Canyon and Mesa Verde. It consists of a circle with groups of rays pointing in four directions – four being a sacred number for the Zia, as it represents the four points of the compass; the four seasons of the year; the four distinct periods of each day; and the four seasons of life. These all are embodied in the earth, bound together in a circle of life and love, without beginning and without end. Zia people believe that the giver of all good gave them gifts in groups of four, and that with life come four sacred obligations: one must develop a strong body, a clear mind, a pure spirit, and a devotion to the welfare of others. At Zia Pueblo, the symbol is painted on ceremonial vases, drawn on the ground around campfires, and used to introduce newborns to the Sun. The symbol on the flag is in red resting on a field of yellow, the colors of old Spain, used by Queen Isabella de Castile.

Fifteen miles northwest of Las Lunas, a **Mystery Rock** bears nine lines of writing composed of Canaanite-Phoenician characters; initially it was thought that the text included Hebrew and Russian Cyrillic letters, and at least one Egyptian and one Etruscan character. Thought to be 2,000 years old, reports of its existence dated back to around 1800. Among those who attempted to decipher it were Dr. Robert H. Pfeifer of the Semitic museum at Harvard University, who in 1949 published an article saying he recognized it as a summary of the Ten Commandments; and Frank Hibben, professor of anthropology at the University of Mexico, thought Mormons had engraved the rock during one of their early migrations across the state. The Archeological Society of Brigham Young University, concerned that the rock would later be shown to be a fraudulent Mormon artifact, sent a team that in 1954 published an article stating that the inscription was quite recent.

In 1954, Albuquerque attorney Robert LaFollette studied the rock, and claimed that a plaster cast he made revealed two faintly drawn human faces that were not discernable to the naked eye on the stone surface. He determined phonetic sounds for the characters, and in reading it aloud thought it sounded like the Navajo language. With the help of a Navajo interpreter he translated it into English, as an account of an epic journey of a people pursued by enemies and fleeing across water; there was an account of a battle and an ordeal of thirst and hunger. The travelers met other tribes, were aided by them, and in the end arrived at a river where they settled. This posed the question, could there actually be a connection between the Navajo language and the Phoenician?

In the late 1970s, Albuquerque resident Dixie L. Perkins saw a program on the Mystery Rock on KOB-TV, insisted that her husband take her to see it – and, four days later, had unraveled the mystery. An epigrapher who had translated 3,500-year-old Cuneiform, and studied Greek and Latin, she was also a professional calligrapher. She identified the letters as being from the Phoenician-Greek alphabet in use in 500 B.C.; all letters were capitals, a style used exclusively in early Greek. The Greek Cypriot letter S, actually two horizontal E's balanced on stems facing each other also appeared; it had been in use in the 4th century B.C., but was not deciphered by scholars until 1910. The Phoenician A did look like a horned cow skull lying on its side ... supplying omitted vowels and translating the resulting Canaanite-Phoenician-Greek message into English, Perkins learned that Zakyneros, the author, was from the Grecian area of the Mediterranean Sea. His poetic saga read: "I have come to this place to stay. The other one met with an untimely death in battle, dishonored, insulted, and stripped of flesh. The men thought him to be an object of care whom I looked after, considered crazed, to be tossed about as if in a wind, to perish in poverty and need. By my kinsmen I was respected and honored, of blessed lot, with a body of slaves and so many olive trees, a peg to hang anything upon. Men punished me with exile to exact retribution for a debt; meanwhile, I remain here as a rabbit. I, Zakyneros, just as a prophet, out of reach of mortal man, I am fleeing and very afraid. I am dross, scum, refuse, just as aboard ship a soft, effeminate sailor is flayed with an animal hide, all who speak offensively are lashed or beaten with a cane; but after a short time, the hurtful ones may be sated; at an unseasonable time, I remain to protect from the rainy southwest winds the hollow or the ravine. Very much harvest is gathered in, very much is in the woody dell and glen; very many bags of young deer. Very many hides with delicate, luxuriant hair; by the channel of a river, swift flowing. Very much is given by the gods, the choicest kind of gift, to call upon the gods for again and again, at the unseasonable time I become gaunt from hunger."

The rock predates Columbus, and the Viking explorations. Whether Zakyneros and his companions, traveling over the Atlantic and across half an unexplored continent to an obscure river known today as the Rio Puerco, built settlements or left other traces of their passage, is still a mystery.

Native American Remains

"My only regret about dying is not being able to see this beautiful country anymore, unless the Indians are right and my spirit will walk here long after I am gone."

– Georgia O'Keefe

Native Americans believed that there were mysterious owners inherent in lakes; spirits in animals, plants, and stones; these had to be propitiated. Zuni *kachinas* pray for rain and good crops from the bottom of a lake near Zuni. Resistance to change carried through in economic and social spheres as well as in the area of religion. Taos Pueblo, for example, held Blue Lake in the Sangre de Cristo Mountains to be sacred, and retained control of it for years rather than ceding it to the federal government, even though this meant that aspects of its religion were revealed to outsiders.

Named for Adolph Bandelier, a nineteenth century anthropologist, Bandolier National Monument was proclaimed on February 11, 1916, and consists of 32,000 acres with 70 miles of trails providing access to hundreds of ruins of Anasazi cliff houses and pueblo-style dwellings, including Tyuonyi village of Frijoles Canyon. A massive stone lion at the crest of a steep-walled mesa near Bandolier and two megaliths next to it remaining from prehistoric times is thought to have been part of a fertility ritual where Indian women once prayed and left offerings of turquoise. Weighing an estimated

1,000 pounds, it is one of the only three bas-relief carvings known to have been created – the other two are side by side within Bandolier National Monument, not far from the Painted Cave.

A team from the University of New Mexico Anthropology Department and the Albuquerque Mountain Rescue Council decided in 1970 to remove the rare sculpture in order to protect it from the elements and from vandalism, placing it in the Maxwell Museum on campus in downtown Albuquerque. They had permission from nearby Cochiti Pueblo to do this – but not the permission of the magical cat itself.

On the day, as the team was ascending with paraphernalia, a solar eclipse took place, and a displaced boulder crushed the leg of one of the team members. Nevertheless the lion was wrapped and bound, ready to be picked up by helicopter – but again, like a jinx, the two volunteers who scrambled down from the mesa and drove by jeep to guide the helicopter pilot in, had the jeep inexplicably run out of gas, and were delayed because, armored in their mountaineering gear, no car would stop and pick them up. The lion was finally lifted off, but when the moment of lowering it to the flatbed truck came, the helicopter lost control of the sculpture, which swung back and forth wildly, smashing out the taillights and bucking the rear wheels off the ground. When the pilot prematurely triggered the release mechanism, the lion fell at a climber's feet, missing his toes by inches. Miraculously, it remained intact.

The lion remained trussed in its wrappings for years, in a corner of the patio at the Maxwell Museum. The people of San Felipe Pueblo claimed the lion as theirs, offended that they had not been asked about moving it; many people at Cochiti Pueblo has not been consulted, and were equally angry. Both demanded that the lion be returned, but the museum refused, on the grounds that the physical protection of the stone was paramount.

It took an Act of Congress – the Native American Religious Freedom Act – to force the lion's return to its resting place, looking out over the canyons carved by the Rio Grande and the Rio Santa Fe, with the snow-clad mountains of the Pecos Mountains rising far to the northeast. To protect it, the exact location is still a well-kept secret.

The two stone lions of Yapashi – Yapashi being a Keresan word for "place of the sacred enclosure" – are surrounded by a circle of stones in Bandolier a steep five miles from Frijoles Creek and the Bandolier parking lot. Worshippers from Cochiti and San Felipe still sprinkle cornmeal on the statues, paint the lions' noses red, and place deer antlers between them, probably continuing an ancient hunting ritual.

Mingled Religions

Don Juan de Oñate led a group of Spaniards, including eight Franciscan priests, into the Estancia Basin only in 1598, attempting to issue and translate the Act of Obedience to the pueblos, who were seeing metal, firearms, horses, and writing for the first time. Oñate kept records, and inscribed names phonetically as signatures to the Act. The colonizers planted a cross near the Rio Grande at a pueblo they called Puaray, halfway between modern Alameda and Sandia, and moved north to establish San Gabriel de Yunque Yunque, near modern San Juan. The first building was a large wooden church, finished in two weeks and named after St. John the Baptist. By 1617, three years before the English landing at Plymouth Rock, there were seven districts and friars claimed to have baptized 8,000 souls, building eleven churches in pueblos they described as "appalling wilderness." Soon there were forty-six "Christian" pueblos.

After years of struggle to govern and economically develop the area, Oñate recommended it be abandoned; but Catholic Spain did not want to give up. Oñate resigned, but New Mexico essentially became a missionary colony, with Franciscans the only religious order. The Estancia Basin was now called the Salinas Province, since the Indians collected salt to trade to other pueblos and the Spaniards. The Spanish civil government demanded tribute in exchange for protection, placing a strain on the livelihood of the Indians, who were forced to help build and maintain missions as well. Believing that work was good for the soul, the Franciscans emphasized labor. They also tended to the sick, established schools, and taught the Indians to grow European crops and build in the European style; thus the Indians learned Spanish, new agricultural methods, architectural techniques, and crafts. Chili was brought in by the Spaniards. Cattle, goats, sheep, horses, and pigs were now kept. Black-on-white pottery took on new forms reflecting European styles. Artifacts of the period include Chinese porcelain, metal tools, and religious medallions.

The Apache had established trading relationships with pueblos on the Rio Grande, and by 1625 had settled west of the river. In 1630 Friar Alonso de Benavides referred to a group of Gila Apaches living in the mountains of west-central New Mexico, and noted that further north "Navajo Apaches" practiced a limited amount of agriculture (these were actually the Dine people, the name later shortened to Navajo). The horse had become highly valued as a beast of burden and source of food, enabling the Apache to increase geographical range and exploit economic resources further afield. By the mid-1700s they had established a network of trading and raiding relationships, made possible through the mobility of the horse.

Native American Ways of Dealing with the Dead

Prehistoric Pecos Pueblo, located eighteen miles southeast of Santa Fe, buried the dead in shallow oval pits in a flexed position, face down; occasionally on the side and rarely on the back. There did not seem to be an orientation to cardinal points. Later, inhumation in an extended position was common.

Hohokam people, desert farmers of the American Southwest based in the middle Gila and Salt River drainage basins in the Sonoran desert of Arizona, in the period 300 B.C. to 1 A.D. traditionally cremated, moving the remains to be placed with shattered vessels in an elongated trench or pit. During the period 1100-1450 A.D., ashes were placed in jars, often with an inverted bowl as a lid. Inhumations began to increase.

Pre-Hispanic desert dwellers of the Cochise culture buried the dead in a flexed position in pits located randomly throughout the village. The Anasazi both cremated and inhumed. Indians believed that departed spirits had the power to make themselves visible and heard, could assume any shape they liked, of animals or men. They would not go near a burial place after dark, and thought that an apparition could strike its beholder with disease; feasts and prayers were done to placate the dead.

Some thought that there was a shade that remained near the body – others, that there was a land where all shades lived together. There might be a ghost that remained near the grave, or places where the person had been in life, disappearing with time.

Many tribes believed evil spirits and troubles were brought upon them by lesser spirits or ghosts not important enough to attract attention from the main god; these included petty malice, vexations and bad luck. They had great faith in their priests and medicine men; as a consequence, the doctor or divining man was punished if he did not produce a cure, as it was thought he was unwilling rather than unable to do so.

Early death was thought to result from witchcraft, unkind thoughts, and/or failure to observe proper ceremonial and sacred rules. Natural death was a transition, another rebirth.

In about 1550 the people at Las Humanas in the Estancia Basin began to cremate their dead, after centuries of burials: Coronado had attacked the Zuni pueblo of Hawikuh in 1540, possibly precipitating the large-scale emigration to Las Humanas. After the 1540s the Zunis cremated the dead with the tools of their occupation.

From 1917 to 1923, excavations at Hawikuh, presently the town of Zuni, cleared some 370 rooms at the village, and dug up nearly 1,000 graves, both cremations and inhumations. Oñate refers to the dead being buried in dirt mounds outside the pueblo of Taos; later Roman Catholic practice prevailed, and they were interred in the courtyard of a church destroyed in 1847, then expanded, gravestones replacing simple wooden crosses.

Picuris Pueblo, located in the mountains of northern New Mexico, had joined the 1680 Revolt: At Picuris Pueblo, located in the mountains of northern New Mexico, in the 1880s the deceased was dressed in traditional clothing, a stripe of black mica drawn on the face, prayer feather placed in the hands. Special death songs were sung. A wake was held with the singing of Christian hymns. In the morning a bag of food was tied at the waist of the body before it was taken out for burial; cedar sprigs were used to sweep the area. Burial was in grounds north of the pueblo. Family members and friends remained at the house of the deceased for four days afterward.

Acoma

Acoma, and the Hopi village of Oraibi in Arizona, are the two oldest continuously occupied settlements in the United States. It was named by Antonio de Espejo's expedition in 1583 from the Keresan words *ako*, meaning white rock, and *mi*, people.

Close to 6,000 pueblo descendents live on the reservation, and over thirty families occupy Sky City, on a sandstone mesa 367 feet above the desert, year round. Once accessible only by climbing a staircase carved out of the rock, a road was paved for a movie company in 1957.

Water was all-important for pueblo villages built along or not far from the Rio Grande River; Acoma, high off the plain, was more dependent upon rain. Many ceremonies focus on the production of rain, which brings fertility to crops – especially corn, symbol of life. Acoma's homes are built of adobe and the local white stone: early windows were made of selenite, an opaque material mined in the area.

In 1598 the pueblo submitted voluntarily to the authority of the Spanish Crown as represented by Don Juan de Oñate; but rebelled in tricking Don Juan de Zaldivar into entering the pueblo to obtain cornmeal, killing him and twelve soldiers. Oñate summoned a weakened Spanish force of seventy men, protected by armor and equipped with guns, who overcame the pueblo after a battle of three days resulting in as many as 800 deaths. Seventy Indian warriors were then murdered and their bodies thrown over the cliff. Sixty young girls were sent to Mexico as slaves; other females remained in New Mexico, along with all males between the ages of twelve and twenty-five, as servants. Each older man had one foot cut off and was in bondage to the Spanish for twenty years.

Due to the hostilities, a church was not established in Acoma until 1629. As Fray Juan Ramirez, the first permanent missionary, approached, a little girl was inadvertently pushed off the top of the cliff and fell upon a pointed rock sixty feet below. Fray Ramirez knelt and prayed beside her, and then carried her up, unharmed; another version of the story has Fray Ramirez catching the girl as she fell, thus earning gratitude instead of hostility. This goodwill was again destroyed during the Pueblo Revolt of 1680, when Fray Lucas Maldonado was murdered, and Acoma remained hostile for over sixteen years. It was the last of the New Mexico pueblos to yield once more to Spanish rule in 1699.

An Acoma Indian was among the seven Pueblo governors who went to Washington in 1863 to meet with President Lincoln and settle boundaries; each were given a silver-headed cane engraved with the inscription "A. Lincoln, Prst. U.S.A., 1863." These canes now constitute the badge of office, being passed to succeeding governors upon election in January.

The church, San Esteban Rey (St. Stephen the King), for which all materials were carried or hauled up and which was built without the use of nails, is the largest structure at Acoma, and is still in use, with walls painted white annually before St. Stephen's feast day. The paint is ground from pink and white stones and applied with traditional yucca and sheepskin brushes. Wooden Stations of the Cross date from the seventeenth century. Originally St. Stephen the Martyr was the patron saint of Acoma, but his feast is December 26, conflicting with Christmas, so St. Stephen, king of Hungary, was chosen to replace him, the feast day being September 2nd.

A burial ground off the patio of the church was created to give Acoma converts a consecrated place in which to bury their dead. A stone retaining wall almost ten feet high was built around the outer edge of the rock, enclosing an area two hundred feet square. Earth from the plain below was carried up, a sackful at a time, to fill it. Deer heads have been carved into the corners of the wall, where hunters prayed; carved soldiers' faces served as guardians of the dead. On All Souls Day and Memorial Day, Acoma families lay gifts of food on the graves.

King Philip II of Spain had made a gift to the church of a painting of St. Joseph, which was believed to have miraculous powers: the Lagunas asked to borrow it in order to stop droughts, epidemics and other calamities, and it was efficacious, but they did not return it. The matter was the subject of a lawsuit fought through the U.S. courts from 1852 to 1857, when, in a drawing of lots at a council of Acoma and Laguna, the slip with a rude sketch of the painting was drawn by a little girl from Acoma Pueblo, and the painting was brought back.

However, one morning soon after its return, the painting had disappeared again. The Acoma were ready to go to war, but their priest advised them to take the matter to District Court at Santa Fe. The decision was for Acoma, but Laguna appealed the case to Supreme Court, where again the decision was in Acoma's favor.

The Acoma committee traveling to retrieve the painting was only halfway to Laguna when they found the painting of St. Joseph under a tree. Their conclusion was that St. Joseph had already learned of the decision and had started to return, but became tired and was resting under the tree when he was met.

Hopi

The Hopi tribe were living in pueblo-style dwellings in northeastern Arizona when the first outsiders arrived; self-sufficient, they had a system of irrigation for crops, but also relied on prayers to supernatural beings or *kachinas*, known as 'cloud people', their spiritual essence manifest as rain. When these ritual figures depart a dance, they are entreated to have mercy with their liquid essence, rain, so that all things may grow and life be bountiful.

Hopi cosmology is composed of four world, or phases of life; they believe themselves to now be in the fourth way, having been offered corn by the creator, Ma'saw, in moving from the third to the fourth, they were reluctant to take it, and were left with the smallest and shortest blue corn. This predicted that their life to come would be difficult. Seeing the earth as a wonderful and giving living spirit, the well-being of which would depend on them as caretakers, they manifest the virtues of cooperation, humility, and respect. The Hopi live in four separate and autonomous mesas or villages, each including sub-communities. Immigrant Tano families from Rio Grande settled at First Mesa, Arizona, in 1700, becoming part of the Hopi.

The Hopi see death as involved in a system of alternation and continuity – the sun in its journey descends into its western home, also the lower world of the dead. Death is birth into a new world, and Hopi burial practices parallel those of birth except that four black lines of charcoal separate the dead from his home in the village, whereas four white lines of cornmeal mark the walls of a newborn's house.

The spirits of the dead could also return to the world as kachinas: dancers emerge from the underground kiva. Prior to burial, the hair of the deceased was washed with a corn ear; the face and body were washed like a baby's with cornmeal. Feathers were tied over the head, and a cotton mask called a 'white cloud' was formed over the face, with a string feather tied to it. The face was partially painted black. This was to make the body light as a cloud, and to give breath for the other world.

Since the essence of the individual is also conceived of as liquid, a Hopi will say, "I have the liquid essence of my fathers" to express kinship. Through rain falling on the earth and its transformation to corn, the blessings of the kachinas become part of the bodies of the living: thus the relationship between cotton masks and clouds, the living and the dead, rain and life.

A prayer stick was made and the individual given a new name for his incarnation in the other world. Water and bread were placed on or near his chest, he was placed in a seated position with pottery bowls, sometimes broken, a basket of prayer sticks, and a planting stick on the grave mound. Women traditionally wailed throughout the ceremony. Shroud clothes and a corncob were kept at the house for four days, after which the spirit of the dead was considered to have departed.

The Hopi crafting of kachina figures from cottonwood root possibly was inspired by Spanish religious carvings. They represent many spirits venerated by the Hopi, human, plant, and animal as well as mythological. Kachinas can be divided into roughly five categories – spirit beings, guards, racers, ogres, and clowns – with spirit beings encompassing every living thing in the Hopi world. Guards protect the kachinas from those whose behavior is inappropriate at the dances, which are religious occasions. Ogres reinforce positive behavior in children. Clowns entertain, to incorporate humor in often-somber dances. Racers reflect the Hopi ability to race from village to village, communicating with friend and foe.

The carvings became commercial, being mass produced and sometimes painted with acrylic as a source of income for the Hopi, until in the 1970s. In the 1970s, there was a return to simple hand crafting and natural color, with prayers offered during the carving, to result in a static piece to hang on a wall. The Hopi community eagerly embraced this return to integrity, and the traditional work has been much collected.

Navajo

The Navajo, or Dine, are the largest Indian nation in the U.S., accounting for fifteen percent of the Native American population as reported in the 1990 U.S. census, with tribal numbers in excess of 250,000. Their name comes from the term the neighboring pueblos used for the area of the Southwest that the people occupied, Navajo; when the Spanish arrived they referred to the Dine people as Apaches de Navajo, which was later shortened to Navajo.

The Navajo were told by medicine men for generations that they were the descendents of earlier folk who had been plants and animals with human characteristics; they emerged into the world from four lower worlds when threatened by a flood, primordial beings moving toward light. In the world of sunlight and understanding, they were given form. Another creation myth has the people meeting pueblo Indians in the Fourth World, who shared with them crops and knowledge of irrigation. Coyote, instigator of mischief and chief antagonist in many Navajo folktales, was also created in the Fourth World. They regard the universe as an orderly, all-inclusive, unitary system of interrelated elements, each having its place and function.

The Navajo tribe developed a distinctive architectural style over the course of centuries, building a Hogan dwelling, a round or polygonal structure usually with one room. The earliest were probably conical, erected with one forked pole holding up two other principal poles, similar to those made by tribes of the Athapascan group in Canada. Smaller poles and brush were placed on the supports, the surface covered with packed earth. A variant has a separate support for a roof, with vertical walls leaning against it. This construction was copied for frontier log cabins. Adobe, cinder block, and frame-stucco hogans have also been developed for sandstone, pine forest or desert scrub surroundings. Though most Navajo families now live in suburban-style frame houses, traditional hogans are maintained for holding ceremonies. Oil-drum stoves have been replaced with cast iron stoves or gas heat.

The Navajo believe that evil complements good: a human who was good in life has an evil component that becomes a dangerous ghost after death. Disturbance of natural harmony or balance, loss of control, these things all lead to harm. Ghosts may be provoked into return by improper burial or disturbance of the grave. It is traditional to burn the hogan after its owner dies; Navajos fear the bodies of the dead. Navajo witches can cause evil by sprinkling corpse powder, obtained from the skin of a dead person, on a person. Sorcerers can cast spells from a long distance by using the victim's clothing or a piece of hair or nail as a substitute for the physical presence. Murder is dangerous not because of the deed itself but because of the contact with the dead.

Ritual is the means of setting things right. The medicine men or women, called singers, perform intricate ceremonies, learning the chants and movements during apprenticeships in which they follow older practitioners. Before one can perform the ritual, one must have someone perform it on him, and must pay for the service.

The Enemyway rite, lasting three or five nights, was used to protect warriors from the ghosts of slain enemies: it has been elaborated as a cure for sickness thought to be caused by the ghosts of non-Navajos. It is an Evilway ritual that may involve exorcism, garment or cincture ceremonies, overshooting, blackening or reddening the patient, and lightning-herb, ash-blowing, and brushing procedures. There may be a ghost's offering of a plume stuck in charcoal or blue glass beads and ashes to appease the ghost and attract it so it may be 'shot'. The patient may spend the night upon a sand painting made that night on buckskin or cloth.

Zuni

The Zunis held the Sun Father and Moonlight-Giving Mother as most important, their sons guarding Zuni from six sacred directions. They also worshipped water, as sustaining crops and life. It was said that when the kachinas came in person, before the impersonation dances began, they always took a woman away with them: if a woman followed a dancer, death resulted.

Any initiate of the Kachina Society would go to Kachina Village after death: if he had owned a mask during life he could take part in the constant dance of Kachina Village, and also come invisibly to Zuni to "stand before" the living kachina impersonators. The Zuni community was ordered like that of Kachina Village, with the same hierarchy. A woman might go to Kachina Village by virtue of marriage, and if so would perform the same task she had in life, preparing feasts for the dancers. Rain priests, water priests, bow or warrior priests, and beast priests performed their functions in the pantheon. Any resident of Kachina Village could return as a cloud, preferably a rain cloud; but one who never went to see the dancers in life would be alone in the sky, and a person who was not "straight" in life would be a 'lying' cloud.

When one had died four times, he would arrive back at the hole where the Zuni first emerged from earth, even further west than Kachina Village: or he would descend to the lowest of four underworlds to where the Zuni originated. He might then return as an animal, the species depending on knowledge attained in life.

The dead person receives personal prayers and offerings when he is first 'sent away from Zuni', but then ceases to be mentioned by name and loses personal individual identity, mentioned only as a member of a group of dead referred to in prayers, ancestors in general, or kachinas.

When a Zuni man's wife died, he underwent four days of observance. He had to be celibate, and could eat no meat, grease or salt. He sat away from the fire and must not be touched.

Each morning he would drink an emetic tea, and offer black corn to the dead: holding it in his hand, he would pass it four times over his head, throwing it away as exorcism. With his right hand, he would scatter white meal and pray. The ritual was also required of a warrior who had taken a scalp, for removal of contamination and propitiation of the ghost.

The ghost of the spouse would be lonely and would try to visit in dreams: the black meal was to 'make the road dark'. After the four days, the bereaved husband would plant prayer sticks.

He would remain celibate for twelve months, so that the dead wife wouldn't be jealous; during this time he was considered "dangerous." At the end of the year, he could have sex with a stranger to whom he would give a gift – she would be the instrument of removing contamination, and would throw away the gift. The next day, both would plant prayer sticks. The period of celibacy could be shortened by asking a man with esoteric knowledge to make especially potent prayer sticks, to be planted at intervals of four days along with special prayers. This ritual also was observed by a warrior who had taken a scalp.

Prayer Sticks

A proper prayer stick had to be found, one not touching the ground; it could touch water, but not earth. It might be hanging from or in a different tree than that of its origin; those in a different tree had more associative ability. It was important to know which tree it was from, and which direction of the tree it separated from, which way it was pointing in the air. Recommended trees were the oak, gum, willow, red cedar, walnut, pecan, and any fruitwoods; the oak was the tree of 'magic' in answering prayers. Prayer sticks made of cedar were to be forked. The maker of the prayer stick had to feel a connection to the tree. Holly, pine, vines, bushes, or any thorny or aggressive trees or plants were not recommended.

The pueblo Indians used sticks of cottonwood about seven inches long, varying in shape, colour, and the feather attached as supplicatory offering to the spirits, according to the nature of the petitions, and the person praying. The stick was intended to represent the god to whom the feathers conveyed the prayers breathed into the spirit of the plumes. Hopi Indians attached a small bag of sacred meal. Green and blue prayer-sticks were found in pueblo graves and used in the ceremonial graves of Arizona.

The bigger end of the prayer stick, attached to its source, was the source of its direction, making it a 'South East' oriented prayer stick if the big end was in the South and the smaller towards the East, for example. The properties of the directions were:

North – Growing and Doing Medicine

East – Flowering and distribution as well as Share and Reflection Medicine

South – Beginning and seed planting as well as Flow and initiating Medicine

West – Sprouting, Metamorphosis, and Give-Away Medicine

Before receiving a thing, something must be given first, so the method was to offer tobacco or a pebble gift on the ground directly beneath the prayer stick before receiving it, preferably with the left hand. Tobacco might be offered to the largest tree of the same species in the area and permission asked to take a part of its relative. Tobacco might also be placed at the tree of origin at the direction of the source, while standing with one's belly and forehead pressed against the trunk, holding hands at heart height, feet at the base. Taking a deep breath, and then exhaling, one projected one's consciousness through the bark and into the heart of the tree until one was able to see the rings of the tree around oneself – and then could travel in spirit form. Light forms might float about in the air, as the tree spirit was asked to allow stripping all bark of the tree and associations with itself. Alternatively, the bark could be carved while on the stick. In releasing the tree, thanks were expressed, and it was asked to provide new, thin, and slippery bark on the tree, representing an Ego more easily stripped.

The length of the prayer stick in some cases was equivalent to the measurement from the maker's elbow to the tips of the fingers. All bark, representing Ego, that was stripped from the prayer stick released its maker from the confinements of Ego. This could be done before or after marrying it to fire, by placing it in an oven at 250 degrees for four hours or by passing it through a flame. One feather, traditionally a wild turkey feather, should be added to the prayer stick, and elements such as embedded crystals and stones in places that the prayer stick told its owner that it wanted them – though some tribes believed that metal or stones were *not* to be tied to the stick. If the stick was forked, a bit of tobacco was placed in a red cloth and tied onto one of the forks. Animal Spirits could be added as well – fur or bone from an animal that the maker wished to honor. It should be smudged with sage or cedar to facilitate renewal, and clear it of past associations, thoughts, and memory.

Any prayer stick could be used to pray for anything, but some achieved the objectives of prayers of desire because of the properties attached to them. The prayer stick could be placed before a shrine in the kiva or buried in the plaza. Prayer sticks might be made by everyone in a family for four days before the solstice, and planted, at least one by each person, on the day of the solstice in small holes dug by the head of the household. Each prayer stick would be named for an ancestor or deity.

Incoming Christianity

The polytheistic Indians had borrowed effective deities from neighboring peoples before, and at first saw Christianity as a logical addition to gods they already had. They could relate to the desert setting of Biblical stories, and to Elijah's competition with the priests of Baal to end the drought. From the Indian point of view, both kiva and church were harmonious.

Quarai

The mission built at Quarai in the early 1600s was witness to the encounter of two vastly different worlds: the earliest attempt to blend European and American Indian cultural traditions. Spanish priests had arrived at the pueblos to establish missions: large stone churches were built and efforts were made to convert the Indians to Christianity and create self-sufficient communities. A kiva, the ceremonial chamber of the pueblo religion, had been there since 1200, well before the church and convent were built. Both square and round kivas are common, the flat roof supported by posts; on the floor was a fire pit, and the hatchway above served as both an entrance and an opening for smoke to escape. As warm air and smoke rose out the hatchway, cool air descended through a ventilator shaft on the east side. Thus fresh air circulated through the kiva, making it a reasonably comfortable place for various activities. Used as chapter, or council, rooms, the Indians met in them to discuss matters of their government for the coming year, sowing, scheduling tasks, to elect new community officials, to rehearse dances, and for rituals. Boys were initiated into the tribe in the kiva between the ages of 7-10. Pueblo ceremonies, whether public or private, took precedence over all other activities.

Medicine societies formed the basis of most tribal political and ceremonial arrangements: the societies named officials each year, and concerned themselves with curing, general well being of all tribe members, and weather control. Kivas were also used as solar markers.

There are variations in the creation stories handed down by elders in the pueblos, but all have in common emergence from a lower world through a hole, the *sipapu*. It is also seen as the womb of the Earth Mother. As water is important in pueblo life – those built high off the plain being even more dependent on rain – water-giving rites induct the infants of San Juan into the tribe, and its creation story has the people emerging from the *sipapu* by way of a lake.

Inhabitants of the Eastern Tewa pueblos of the Rio Grand Valley believed that men, gods, and animals all lived together in the underworld where life began, when the upper world was 'unripe', formed of mist and haze. As it hardened, the inhabitants of the lower sphere emerged, and two men were chosen as leaders: one for the Summer People, one for the Winter. The Summer People went south on the west side of the Rio Grande, the Winter People to the east. Both groups met at Ojo Caliente, founding the five Tewa villages of San Juan, Santa Clara, San Ildefonso, Nambe, and Tesuque. The ancient people emerged into the new world feeling a sense of reverence and love for what was left behind, and fear and respect for what they faced. Spirits guided them, and within communities they were reminded of their shared past and told how to work together for the good of the community and the necessary harmony with the universe. To achieve these, the complex ceremonial system evolved, directed by priests.

Santo Domingo and other Keresan communities emphasize the position of the Corn Mother, Iyatiko, in the role of 'Bringing to Life'.

She remains at the *sipapu* or emergence place, but is represented in ceremonies by a perfect ear of corn, the symbol of fertility. For Zia or Cochiti pueblos, Spider Woman or Thinking Woman holds a more central place. The Indian New Year begins after harvest in October, with ceremonies at winter solstice or the 'turning-back-of-the-sun'. At the spring equinox prayers for the summer growth, fertility, and rain take over.

Since the kiva is buried by mission construction, this implies that the Spanish structures were built on a mound of pueblo ruins. The kiva at Quarai was never in use during the mission period. The architectural contrast between native and Spanish structures is clear; and it suggests an even greater gulf between the social and spiritual worlds of the cultures that created them.

Fray Francisco Letrado had arrived with the 1629 supply train, and began a church at Las Humanas, first taking over and remodeling eight abandoned Indian rooms. One was a small chapel. When these temporary quarters were ready, Letrado began work on a large, permanent church, cutting into the hillside at what was to be the altar end. He had just begun work on the walls when he was transferred at his request to Zuni – and was martyred there the following spring. It seems that he had interrupted an Indian ceremony to urge the people to mass. In retribution, a military force was sent from Santa Fe, marking their passing on a rock called El Morro as many other travelers had, by carving graffiti into the soft sandstone.

Letrado was not replaced, but Fray Acevado, who had accompanied him when he came, completed the small church, though the village could not support a major mission (Las Humanas was renamed Gran Quivira, for the treasure Coronado had searched for in 1540, sometime after 1848 when the Salinas became part of the United States). Acevedo then continued his work at Abó, renovating and rebuilding San Gregorio de Abó. Ruins of all three missions are preserved at Salinas Pueblo Missions National Monument.

In Spanish-Indian relationships, Spain's sophisticated legal system was intended to protect the Indians' civil and property rights; and perhaps Spanish colonists learned the patience and endurance that had been practiced in the pueblos for centuries. The Apaches, on the other hand, were always on the move; the Spaniards saw them as 'uncivilized' and made slaves of them. Though historically the Apaches had maintained a good trading relationship with the pueblos, they now felt that a Spaniard was a Spaniard, all were enemies, and a friend of the enemy was an enemy as well. The wagon trains that brought supplies and returned with cargoes of woolen cloth, buffalo, and antelope skins, piñon nuts, and salt, now began to carry back Indian slaves, which enraged the Franciscans. The conflict came to a head in the early 1660s and is documented in Inquisition records. Clashes between the rulers on allegiance to God and church or king undermined their hold.

During the New Mexico Inquisition in the 1600s, three of Quarai's Spanish held high positions, including Fray Estevan de Perea, Custodian of the Franciscan order in the Salinas Jurisdiction, named by one historian 'Father of the New Mexican Church'. Records show that unlike the perpetrators of the horrors of the Spanish Inquisition, these were compassionate men, usually capable of separating gossip from what the church regarded as serious transgressions.

Quarai, where past inhabitants still appear

Tensions did peak when Perea charged the *alcalde* (mayor) of Salinas with encouraging the native kachina dances: the case was dropped, but the *alcalde's* continued interference at the mission prompted the Inquisition to banish him.

> Inasmuch as I have had word that at the pueblo of Pecos a partially subterranean room in the form of a kiva or *coi* [a kiva within a house block] has been built apart from the pueblo under the pretext of the women getting together to spin; inasmuch as its door should open on the street, and the king our lord (God save him) has ordered all his ministers to observe with utmost diligence that such rooms are not built in the pueblos because of the great superstitious and idolatrous abuses that are committed, as is of record; and inasmuch as there are in addition to this one others in said pueblo, I order the *alcalde* mayor of that district to go immediately and ascertain if it is true. If it is, he will make them destroy and demolish it immediately.

Gov. Juan Ignacio Flores Mogollón,
Santa Fe,
January 20, 1714

When drought set in, the Apaches raided the pueblos, and disease also became rife. Hunger finally drove both Spaniards and Indians from the Salinas, Quarai pueblo being abandoned during the 1670s, a calamity foreshadowing the 1680 revolt.

At Quarai in 1913, visitors to the ruins saw a blue-white light glowing through an opening in the adobe wall near the choir loft. A Spanish soldier wearing a tabard emblazoned with a large red cross, symbol of the military religious order of Calatrava, stood in the center of the space pointing his finger at the tourists and said, "Siste, viator," which means 'stop, visitor' in Latin. However, in antique Spanish it may have been 'Asiste, viador', meaning 'attend, or frequent this place, traveler on a mystic journey'. The language and the uniform of the soldier place him in the sixteenth century, when the mission was still active. He has never appeared again.

The abandoned land at Quarai

Native American Rituals

Most Apache deities personified natural forces; some animals and birds were intrinsically dangerous. But Coyote, source of trouble, is also the bringer of fire to men. Their religion is rich with myths, spirits, and ghosts. Yusn, Giver of Life and Source of Power, and White Painted Woman, corresponding to the Navajo Changing Woman, share the world with other beings that have powers. The use of masked impersonators of the gods suggests pueblo influence, as does incorporating sand painting in rituals. Apaches use the same sacred colors as the Navajos and the pueblos, but associate them with different directions, such as with black representing east instead of north. Some ceremonies of the Jicarilla are strikingly similar to those of the Navajo.

'Kan' was the term for the principal Apache gods; their appearance in rituals and the tail of the hat worn suggest a centipede, an important animal god. An Apache or medicine man in full regalia was no longer a man, but became the power he represented. An Apache related to one of the Spaniards that they used to "watch the kan come down the hill;" Mexicans had also cried, "Here come our gods" of the masked and disguised priests, especially when they had "donned the skins of the women offered up in sacrifice." (Annual Report of the Bureau of American Ethnology) Spanish writers described the headdresses as 'miters', leading to some confusion when one Apache speaking through a translator introduced himself as a bishop.

Sorcery was accomplished by 'shooting' substances, sometimes bits of bone and hair of the dead, into the victim: the curing rite involved locating and extracting the 'arrow' of the witch. Apaches believed sorcerers were also liable to be incestuous; anyone charged with incest was also automatically treated as a witch.

The number four is special: many ceremonies last four days or nights, and rituals are performed in sets of four. In the puberty ritual of the Mescaleros, men representing the Mountain Spirits arrive in fours, and the girls are grouped in fours.

At the time of death, the Apache believed a ghost was released that could harm the living unless it promptly went to the afterworld and stayed there: a dead kinsman was believed to appear to the dying in order to lead him on the four-day journey north to reach the desired afterworld destination. Protective measures were taken against the ghost returning. Returning ghosts would be lonely. Close relatives went into mourning, wearing old clothes and cutting the ends of their hair. The young were especially susceptible to ghosts; only the elderly washed the body, combed the hair, and dressed the deceased in fine clothes.

Burial was in daytime and as soon as possible. Navajo, Western Apache, and Kiowa-Apache removed the corpse through a hole broken in the sidewall, not through the door. The body was placed on a favorite horse, along with personal possessions, and taken far from the dwelling places of people, into the hills or mountains if possible. The accompanying party was small, and tribes-people encountered turned away. The grave was a crevice in rock, covered with earth, brush, and stones. Some personal possessions were buried, others were broken and left at the site; the horse was killed there, for use in the afterworld. The party returned by a different route, without looking back, and not discussing the location. Clothes that had been worn for the burial were discarded, and participants took a ritual bath, using ashes on themselves and scattering them around the camp to discourage the return of the ghost.

In the home of the deceased, personal possessions were broken or burned, including possessions of others that the dead person had used or handled frequently. Nothing should remain to remind one of the dead, because thinking of him would attract the ghost. His name was not spoken again. The encampment was moved, if only to a nearby location as a symbolic move. The mourning relatives were isolated for a time.

Ghosts were thought to come at night, in human guise or as black shapes – they could use an owl or coyote as a vehicle. They whistled to frighten people; therefore, whistling at night was frowned upon. Navajo and Kiowa-Apache believed that a ghost could return in the form of a whirlwind. Children were especially vulnerable to attention from ghosts, and the footprints in soft earth made by a child learning to walk were erased.

Both ghosts and witches could persecute those who angered them; sometimes ghosts were described as the shades of witches who perhaps had not been recognized as such in life. If someone who died had been angry with someone, it was a cause for anxiety. The underworld was divided in two, with a pleasant side for the good and a cheerless and barren one for those who had been witches.

Redefining New Mexico

After the Pueblo Revolt

In the Pueblo Revolt of 1680, the Spaniards who had occupied Native American lands for over eighty years were overthrown. Total Hispanic residents did not exceed three thousand; more than four hundred were killed and churches desecrated, as well as twenty-one of the province's thirty-three Franciscans slaughtered. There were more Spanish settlers living in the present day Albuquerque area than in Santa Fe: about 120 were killed, and survivors driven far south to the crossing of the Rio Grande called 'the pass to the north or El Paso del Norte – modern-day El Paso.

In this general exodus of Indians and Spaniards fleeing drought, the Piro and Tompiro survivors of the Salinas pueblos also moved south to become absorbed by Indian communities in the El Paso area, making them the only linguistic group among the pueblo Indians of the time to lose both their language and their homeland.

In 1692 Don Diego Vargas led another expedition in to reclaim the territory for Spain; this area was important as it served as a buffer against other European powers whose colonies in North America were rapidly expanding toward Spain's possessions. This time the Spanish were more tolerant, seeking to integrate the pueblos into the empire. By the seventeenth century, enough Spanish settlers had returned to populate and name an area Bosque Grande de San Francisco Xavier. They filtered north and reoccupied the Rio Grande Valley, but the increasing presence of the Apache delayed resettlement of the Salinas. In 1750, Governor Toms Velez Cachupin sent troops to temporarily occupy Quarai and Abo, both of which had springs and were close to travel routes. But the pueblo people never returned to the Salinas. Mysterious glowing balls of light seen floating about the ruins of the mission have been described as vestiges of lantern lights from a previous caretaker, while others suggest that they are phantom torches carried by the ghosts of the Spanish missionaries.

The Spanish also set out to subdue the Apache by giving them gifts of cloth, food, inferior firearms and alcohol when they agreed to settle in villages, thus making them subservient and inoperative. This worked with moderate success until after 1821, when Mexican independence was achieved, and the government could not afford to subsidize the rationing system. In 1831 the Apache resumed intensive raiding.

With the opening of the Santa Fe Trail in 1821, trappers, traders, explorers, and other travelers, predominantly French Canadians and Anglo-Americans, began filtering into the area. On August 18, 1846, Brigadier General Stephen Watts Kearny claimed New Mexico as a territory of the United States. Its boundaries were established by 1863, following the Treaty of Guadalupe Hidalgo, the Gadsden Purchase, and several Congressional bills. Only after the railroads were completed between 1878-1911 and the nomadic Indians were subdued did Anglos arrive in large numbers.

The Salinas Province began to be homesteaded in about 1900, after active advertising by the Territory of New Mexico, which was eager for immigration. The new settlers came from Texas and Arkansas, which were experiencing hard times, and developed large dry-land farming operations, raising pinto beans.

Santisima Trinidad Crucificado, *bulto* by Arthur Lopez

The Ghost Dance

Jack Wilson was descended of a family of prophets and shamans and known as a medicine man, called Wovoka among the Paiute, until his adoption of an Anglo name. He experienced a vision during a solar eclipse on January 1, 1889, which inspired the development of the movement known as the Ghost Dance. He prophesied a peaceful end to white American expansion while preaching messages of clean living, an honest life, and cross-cultural cooperation. Beliefs of this movement included that the white man would disappear from the Earth after a natural catastrophe and that the Indian dead would return, bringing with them the old way of life that would then last forever.

This was not Jack Wilson's first time experiencing a vision directly from God; he had received training from an experienced shaman under his parents' guidance after they realized that he was having difficulty interpreting his previous visions. He now claimed that he was older and better equipped, spiritually, to handle the message. Jack was also training to be a 'weather doctor' like his father and was known throughout the valley as a gifted and blessed young leader.

The Ghost Dance was a religious movement incorporated into numerous Native American belief systems. The traditional ritual of the circle or round dance, symbolizing the sun's heavenly path across the sky, was a community dance centered around an individual who leads the ceremony, often accompanied by trance, exhortations, and prophesying. It has been used since prehistoric times, but was first performed in accordance with Jack Wilson's teachings among the Nevada Paiute in 1889, then sweeping throughout much of the American West, to reach areas of California and Oklahoma. Unlike other Indian dances with fast steps and loud drumming, the Ghost Dance involved slow, shuffling movements; it was performed for four or five days and was accompanied by singing and chanting, but no drumming or other musical instruments. Both men and women participated in the dance, unlike others in which men were the main dancers, singers, and musicians. An essential doctrine of the new religion was the brotherhood of man, and as a consequence of this no acts or ceremonies of a warlike nature were included. Tribes incorporated selective aspects of the ritual with their own beliefs. Anthropologist Leslie Spier, a student of Franz Boas, noted that most of these 'prophet dances' had already incorporated Christian elements.

Northern Paiutes living in Nevada were foragers for food and lacked a political organization or officials, operating within a social system of self-proclaimed spiritually blessed individuals who organized events and activities for the group as a whole. Usually these centered on the observance of a ritual at a prescribed time of year or consisted of activities like harvests or hunting parties. In 1869, Hawthorne Wodziwob had organized a series of community dances to announce his vision, speaking of a journey to the land of the dead and of promises made to him by the souls of the recently deceased, who promised to return to their loved ones within a period of three to four years. His peers accepted this vision since he was a popular healer, and danced the circle dance as was customary during a festival. He had continued preaching his message for three years, assisted by a local "weather doctor," the father of Jack Wilson.

A devastating typhoid epidemic had struck in 1867, with other European diseases killing approximately one tenth of the total population, which brought widespread psychological and emotional trauma and grave disorder in the economic system. The introduction of the horse had also revolutionized the foraging lifestyle. Many could not continue their nomadic lifestyle, following pine nut harvests and wild game herds, and ended up in Virginia City seeking wage work.

Jack told anthropologist James Mooney in 1892 that he had stood before God in Heaven, had seen many of his ancestors happily engaged in a beautiful land filled with wild game, and had been instructed to tell his people that they must love each other, not fight, and live in peace with the whites – work, not steal or lie, not engage in the old practices of war or the traditional self-mutilation practices connected with mourning the dead. By following these rules they would be united with their friends and family in the other world. There would be no sickness, disease, or old age. Jack was commanded to take the Ghost Dance back to his people, and preached that if the five-day dance was performed in proper intervals, the performers would achieve happiness and hasten the reunion of the living and deceased. Jack was also given powers over weather and told that he would be the deputy in charge of affairs in the Western United States, with President Harrison as God's deputy in the East.

While one of the primary goals of the Bureau of Indian Affairs was to convert the Indians to Christianity, they did not recognize that the basis of the Ghost Dance was Christian in nature and converted many to a belief in the Christian God. Wovoka – also called 'the brown-skinned Messiah' – preached that, to survive, the Indians needed to turn to farming and to send their children to school to be educated, efforts that coincided with the goals of the Bureau.

Paiute brethren dubbed the new practice 'Dance In A Circle'; because the first Anglo contact came by way of the Sioux, their expression 'Spirit Dance' was adopted for all such rituals, subsequently translated as 'Ghost Dance'. The message spread across much of the western portion of the United States. Mormons from Utah, for whom the concepts of the Native American prophet were familiar and often accepted, and many tribes sent members to investigate; other communities sent delegates just to be cordial – those who left as believers returned preaching the message. While most saw Wovoka's role as being that of a teacher of pacifism and peace, others did not.

The Sioux used hypnosis to bring about trances to aid in the communication with the dead, and a 'Ghost Shirt', believed to hold spiritual power; observers such as James Mooney believed that the most likely basis is the Mormon endowment 'garment' to protect the pious wearer. Made of buckskin or cloth, the purpose of the shirt was to make the wearer immune to bullets, a weapon of death known initially only to the white man. Chief Kicking Bear brought the concept to his Lakota Sioux in 1890, who interpreted Jack's religion as the idea of a "renewed Earth" in which 'all evil is washed away' by removal of all Anglo Americans from their lands, though his version encouraged harmonious coexistence.

During this apocalypse the earth would be destroyed, only to be recreated with Indians as the inheritors of the new earth; the recent times of suffering had been brought about by their sins. They needed to purge themselves of the evil ways learned from the white man, especially the drinking of alcohol. Believers should engage in frequent ceremonial cleansing, meditation, prayer, chanting, and, most importantly, dance the Ghost Dance. They had withstood enough under the whites, who would be obliterated; new spring soil would cover the land and restore the prairie, the buffalo and antelope would return, and deceased ancestors would rise to once again roam an earth free of violence, starvation, and disease. A natural balance would be restored, the land open, without the borders and boundaries of the white man. Hearing rumors of the prophecy and fearing violence, homesteaders panicked and the government responded.

In February 1890, the United States government broke a Lakota treaty by adjusting the Great Sioux Reservation of South Dakota, previously encompassed the majority of the state, into five smaller reservations to accommodate white homesteaders from the Eastern United States, in accordance with the government's clearly stated 'policy of breaking up tribal relationships' and 'conforming Indians to the white man's ways, peaceably if they will, or forcibly if they must'. On the reduced reservations, tribes were separated into family units on 320 acre plots, forced to farm, raise livestock, and send their children to boarding schools that forbade any inclusion of Native American traditional culture and language. The plan failed to take into account the difficulty Sioux farmers would have in trying to cultivate crops in the semi-arid region; by the end of the 1890 growing season, a time of intense heat and low rainfall, the land was clearly unable to produce substantial agricultural yields. Simultaneously the government's patience with supporting Indians ran out, resulting in rations being cut in half.

Increased performances of the Ghost Dance ritual ensued, frightening the supervising agents of the BIA. The Sioux variation on the Ghost Dance tended towards millenarianism, distinguishing it from Jack Wilson's original teachings. Agent McLaughlin asked for troops, claiming that Hunkpapa spiritual leader Sitting Bull, who had been forced to leave the Standing Rock Indian Resevation, was the real leader of the movement. Notorious as the chief who led his people on a frightful journey to Canada, and then, four years older and starving, returned, Sitting Bull had been a celebrity in Buffalo Bill's Wild West Show. A former agent, Valentine McGillycuddy, saw nothing extraordinary in the dances and ridiculed the panic that seemed to have overcome the agencies, saying: "The coming of the troops has frightened the Indians. If the Seventh-Day Adventists prepare the ascension robes for the Second Coming of the Savior, the United States Army is not put in motion to prevent them. Why should not the Indians have the same privilege? If the troops remain, trouble is sure to come."

Thousands of additional U.S. Army troops were deployed and on December 15, 1890, forty-three Indian police, backed up by a squadron of cavalry three miles away, surrounded Sitting Bull's cabin before dawn to arrest him for failing to stop his people from practicing the Ghost Dance. Sitting Bull asked that his horse be saddled as he dressed. When they left the cabin, a group of Ghost Dancers much larger than the police force had assembled; one dancer pulled out a rifle and shot the lieutenant in the side. In an attempt to shoot back, the lieutenant accidentally shot Sitting Bull, and another policeman shot Sitting Bull in the head. Many Indian police died before the cavalry arrived to quell the fighting.

A Miniconjou leader named Big Foot, on the U.S. Army's list of trouble-making Indians, was stopped en route to convene with the remaining Sioux chiefs. Big Foot was forced with his people by the U.S. Army to relocate to a small camp close to the Pine Ridge Agency, so that the soldiers could keep an eye on him. On December 28, the small band of Sioux set up tipis on the banks of Wounded Knee Creek. The following day, as officers attempted to collect weapons from the band. One young and deaf Sioux warrior refused to relinquish his; in the struggle that followed, someone's weapon discharged into the air. A U.S. officer gave the command to open fire, and the Sioux responded by taking up previously confiscated weapons; U.S. forces responded. The Wounded Knee massacre in 1890 resulted in the deaths of 25 U.S. soldiers, many killed by friendly fire, and at least 153 Lakota Sioux, most of whom were women and children.

Chief Kicking Bear officially surrendered his weapon following the massacre to General Nelson A. Miles. Outrage in the Eastern United States emerged, since the U.S. government had insisted on numerous occasions that the Native American had already been successfully pacified, and it was felt the U.S. Army actions had been harsh. Public uproar played a role in the reinstatement of the previous treaty's terms, including full rations and more monetary compensation for confiscated lands.

Ghost Dance in the Southwest

The Walapai of northwest Arizona borrowed the motif of the Ghost Dance from 1889-1895, using it as an emotional alternative for their desire to remove Anglos from the territory, allowing a return to previous subsistence patterns, and for the resurrection of dead ancestors. It was understood that these goals were to be achieved through magical means: no military action was taken against them.

The Apache Spirit Dance was done on momentous occasions such as setting out on war parties, dealing with epidemics, or other things of portent. Feathers of the eagle were worn to conciliate the powerful bird; turkey feathers were an appeal to the mountain spirits; white gull feathers were for water. Bodily decoration included snakes, a bear pattern, zigzag lightning; a mask might be of a mountain lion.

Apache Ghost Dance headdress, tiara-like, symbolized the sun, the rainbow, stars and lightning, clouds and raindrops, snakes and snake heads – the latter in vertical slats represented hail. A wand like a sword/lath in each hand was ornamented with blue snake-lightning; cuts and thrusts were made to drive malignant spirits away. If the dance was done for an ailing human, the cardinal points were occupied and faced. The dance could continue for four nights – it was bad luck to stop before the fuel was consumed.

Creating Religious Infrastructure

After the bloody Pueblo Revolt, several groups of Spanish colonists had settled in the northwestern section of the fertile Chimayó Valley, considered a sacred place as far back as the creation myths of the Tewa Indians due to the curative powers of its magic soil. When the Twin War Brothers killed the evil giant Yeitso, it was said that they created the hot springs of New Mexico, always a draw for their medicinal qualities. But by now the springs had dried, leaving a pit of mud.

The area was administered by a priest from San Juan Pueblo; the Plaza of San Burenaventura, now called the Plaza del Cerro, built around 1740, the last surviving Spanish fortified plaza in the southwest with the *acequia madre*, or main irrigation ditch, running through the plaza. Early settlers lived in near-total isolation from the mainstream of Spanish colonial authority, centered in Santa Fe; they gradually evolved their own rituals and customs.

The Penitentes

When the Apaches cut the connection of the pueblos to the church, and the priests left, there was no one left to perform Christian ceremonies. The **Penitentes** were a way back to religion. A secret society that existed for years, especially in areas of New Mexico remote from railroads and modern influences, composed almost exclusively of men of Hispanic descent of the Catholic faith; it provided the practical organization behind important observances and made available an appropriate physical setting, including singers and readers, for those who wished to worship. Geographically it was confined to the northerly half of the State, principally to the counties of Taos, Colfax, Rio Arriba, Mora, San Miguel, Sandoval, and Valencia. It also extended into the southern counties of Colorado, which were settled from New Mexico and constituted a part of it until included within the boundaries of the Centennial State organized in 1876.

The original Penitentes are thought to be a survival of the Flagellantes who flourished in various parts of Europe in the Middle Ages, making their first appearance in Italy in 1210. The fundamental principle was that sin could only be expiated by suffering, and forgiveness most surely obtained by self-inflicted torture. St. Justin of Padua reported that this religious frenzy first appeared in Perugia, and soon spread to nearly all of Italy. Old and young from all ranks of life joined the processions, many half clad, carrying scourges made of leather thongs with which they lashed their backs until they were covered with blood, while weeping and imploring the forgiveness of God for all their sins. At night they rushed with lighted candles into churches, prostrating themselves before the altar in an agony of grief and contrition. Despite civil and ecclesiastical authorities frowning upon the movement, it only increased in intensity. In 1260 a hermit of Perugia named Ranier organized the movement, and soon Flagellantes numbering ten thousand marched through the country bearing banners and crosses, spreading across the Alps into Switzerland and Germany with followers in Alsace, Bohemia, and Poland. The raging of the plague in Germany in 1349 increased zeal and the extravagance of actions: The Chronicle of Albert of Strasburg reports that a crowd coming to a public place would place themselves within a circle drawn on the ground and strip, leaving only a breech cloth on. They walked with arms outstretched like a cross around and around the circle, fell prostrated and rose to strike their neighbor with a knotted scourge having four iron points, accompanied by the singing of hymns.

They have been variously called the Fraternity of the Flagellantes, The Brotherhood of the Blood of Christ, the Brothers of the Cross, the Penitent Brothers or simply Los Hermanos (The Brothers), in New Mexico. Pope Clement VI issued a bull against them, and the German bishops forbade them to assemble. This was somewhat effective, but in 1414 a leader appeared, named Conrad, who claimed to have a divine revelation commending the practice of public flagellation, and preached that there was no salvation but by a baptism of blood through the institution of scourging. At one time the Inquisition took action against the sect and ninety-one members were burned at Sangerhusen; the cult soon became active again. Flagellantes were found in all southern Europe during the next century, holding processions during certain festivals in Italy, Spain, and Portugal.

Penitente procession, *bulto* by Arthur Lopez

It is thought that the principles and practices of the society were brought across the ocean to New Mexico; or that they are a continuation and survival of the Third Order of St. Francis. In 1630, Benavides, head of the Franciscan order in New Mexico, quoted to the king an American Indian shaman opposed to Christianity: "You Spaniards and Christians are crazy and desire us to be so also. You are so crazy that you go along through the streets lashing yourselves like madmen, shedding blood," to which Benavides adds: "He must have seen some disciplinary procession of Holy Week, in some Christian Pueblo."

The bishop of Durango, Mexico, pressed for Episcopal jurisdiction and was granted it in 1797; village churches in Albuquerque, Santa Fe, Santa Cruz, and El Paso were secularized by priests answering to Durango. After Mexico declared independence from Spain in 1821, the friars lost royal financial support and had withdrawn almost completely by 1840. In New Mexico, the Penitentes became a folk religion, meeting spiritual and social needs. Between 1790 and 1850, they fulfilled the need for spiritual solace, performing the rites of baptism, confirmation, matrimony, and burial needed for collective survival, though they never performed the Sacraments, until the Roman Catholic Church again became established.

The hierarchy of male members was somewhat like that of siblings in a traditional Hispanic family, in which older siblings had quasi-parental authority and younger siblings were expected to submit. The Hermano Mayor held highest authority, elected annually and responsible for the overall functioning of the organization, meetings, and observances, each individual member, and even for fulfilling certain community expectations. He had considerable power and high status. Occasionally there was a *Hermano Segundo* to assist him. Other offices were usually *Celador* (Warden), *Secretario* (Clerk), *Mandatorio* (Agent, sometimes called Collector or Treasurer), *Maestro de Novios* (Examiner and Teacher of the Novices), *Sangrador* or *Picador* (Blood-letter, or Pricker), *Rezador* (Reader of prayers and rituals), *Coadjutor* (Assistant who washed the whips and attended to wounds), *Enfermo* (Nurse), and *Pitero* (Piper) – the latter *never* played the *pito*, the homemade flute used as accompaniment for various services, for pleasure. *Ayudantes* or *Acompañadores* (Helpers or Attendants), representing Simon the Cyrenian, were appointed to accompany, and if necessary aid, each whipper and cross-bearer.

Men had to have the consent of parents and/or spouse before being admitted to the Brotherhood, and took an oath pledging secrecy and loyalty. Initiation took place during Holy Week; full membership was attained only after several years of penitential activities, and could be revoked for various misdeeds. Membership could not be regained if expulsion had followed conviction, but otherwise could be redeemed through penitential exercises. A Brother of Light who wished to perform a severe penance had to ask permission of the *Hermano Mayor*.

Women served as auxiliaries in preparing meals, caring for the sick, helping at wakes or vigils, and following public processions. Their penances were private, and might be crawling to the *Calvario* on their knees or walking with rice in their shoes.

Moradas, houses in which the Penitentes held their meetings, were usually plain adobe buildings with no windows, and only one small door as an entrance. Above the door, upon the flat roof, a simple cross was the only sign that the building was dedicated to religious purposes. Sometimes Moradas were built in the outskirts of a village, or on an adjacent roadside, in plain view with no attempt at secrecy; others were in one side of a deep arroyo or cañon, in a bend that cut it off from casual observation. In a rocky locality, the morada might be built of stone. A style of architecture evolved from these.

Hymns were long, in the form of the predominate type of Spanish poetry, the eight-syllable verse quatrain with second and fourth lines assonant or rhymed, and were inscribed into private copybooks for safekeeping. There were local variations. They were sung *a capella*, sometimes accompanied by the *pito*, by a *cantador* or a recognized village singer. The Brothers would join in singing the chorus during Penitente observances.

St. Francis of Assisi had established the First Order, the Friars Minor, with rules approved by Pope Innocent III in 1210, and a Second Order, the Sisters of Clare or Poor Clares, in 1212. He is said to have developed the idea of a Third Order, composed of laymen, while preaching in Cannara, where the entire village desired to abandon their homes and become disciples. The Rule of the Third Order was approved by Pope Nicholas IV in 1289. Members of the First Order attended meetings and took part in devotional exercises; those of the Second could hold office; and those of the Third were obligated to practice voluntary punishment.

The Third Order, popular among the people of New Mexico during the Spanish era, sought to carry the principles of St. Francis of Assisi into the life of the laity; for two centuries nearly every leading citizen became a member, evident from reading wills made during that period, nearly all of which stated that the testator was a member. Members had the right to wear the modified Franciscan habit at special masses and during Holy Week; they were buried in the Franciscan habit and white cord, though technically the Order ceased to have canonical existence when the Franciscans withdrew, and many requested burial *sin cajon* (without a casket). Order rules directed that the funeral should be of modest character.

Religious plays (*autos sacramentales*) had become well established in Spain by the fifteenth century, and flowered in the sixteenth and early seventeenth centuries: in the New World Franciscan missionaries had composed these in native languages or translated and adapted Spanish ones for evangelization and instruction. It is likely that the Penitentes appropriated portions of such *autos* for their passion plays. Worship for them was characterized by realistic enactment, intimate participation, and belief in salvation through bodily penance. Penance is one of the four Church Sacraments instituted by Christ.

Preceding Easter, all members were marked with a deeply cut cross on the back, the wound kept open for forty days, until Good Friday. The Brothers met on Ash Wednesday and every Friday during Lent: public recitations of the Stations of the Cross were held, and at night there might be a private flagellant procession. On special days the morada chapel would be open to all worshippers, and services might be held. The requirement of at least annual Confessions and Communion was usually met during this time. All members reopened the cross and kept it open. During Holy Week, the last week in Lent, special exercises increased in intensity, especially from Wednesday through Holy Thursday, to culminate on Good Friday. The Brothers spent most of Holy Week in the morada, doing penances, sleeping on the floor, and eating food that was brought in to them. *Mayordomos* (Stewards) were assigned to provide meals; these were not necessarily members, and other religious persons in the community, including women, often prepared food as a pious act. The men would not return home until officers for the following year had been elected, either after the *Tinieblas* (Eathquake) ceremony or on the morning of Holy Saturday.

On Holy Tuesday novices and those Brothers who wished to do active penance participated in a ritual involving a recited interchange between the brothers within and the penitents without; the penitent would don *calzones*, white cotton trousers, the *Sangrador* would administer the six gashes of the *obligación*, and the penitent would beg forgiveness from the assembled members. The gashes were cut with *pedernales*, flints – sharp stones or pieces of glass; they did not affect musculature, but assured a free flow of blood so that scourgings would not cause welts and bruises. Sometimes offended members gave token lashes, but usually the *Celador* administered suitable discipline. The Hermano Major granted permission for penitential exercises, which were severe but were not intended to be suicidal: a penitent might call for lashes from the *Sangrador* equivalent to the three meditations of the Passion, the five wounds of Christ, His seven last words, the forty days in the wilderness, or others, though he rarely remained conscious for the duration. Finally the *Coadjutor* would bathe the wounds in an astringent of *romarillo* (silver sage).

Those punishing themselves publicly wore only the white *calzones* and a black *venda* (hood) over the face – this more to ensure humility than to hide from authorities. There was the penance of carrying a cross, made of roughly hewn logs of pine of great weight, the largest often measuring over seventeen feet in length. The end with the cross piece was placed on the naked shoulder of the penitent, and with the other end dragging on the ground was borne to a designated point, usually the top of a hill, which represented Calvary. A rough road through stones and other obstructions was selected. Deaths of exhaustion sometimes resulted. Timbers for the *maderos* had been cut when sap began to rise, making the stripping of bark easier; often the huge crosses were left outside the morada through all weather.

Good Friday crucifixions took place in front of the morada; there is no evidence that nails were used, the arms were bound to the shoulder, legs to the thighs, with ropes. At times three men were crucified, representing the two thieves and the Christ. Death did sometimes result from this rite, but not as frequently as portrayed in sensationalized accounts. Those who survived the supreme test were revered and politically powerful thereafter, and if they did not, they earned places in heaven for themselves and their families. It was rumored that the relatives of those who died in this manner were notified when his shoes were placed on their threshold, and that the grave remained secret for one year after his demise; some also claimed that the body was buried upright, or that a large cross and pile of rocks marked the spot.

Scourges were made of a braided rope of yucca (soap weed) or cactus, ending in a knot or ball of cactus; Penitentes threw the cord first over one naked shoulder and then the other, so that the thorny ball struck the same place in the middle of the back, turning it to a mass of gore. This ritual took place sometimes within the morada and sometimes in procession, accompanied by musicians who kept up a continual chant, and with followers to support the suffering in case they fell or fainted.

And there was a kind of hand-cart or wheelbarrow with two small wheels, which easily sank to their centers; in this a skeleton with a human skull, filled with stones and bones that represented daily penance, also adding weight – this may be a remnant of the death carts of the Plague. It was drawn by lines of cord over the shoulders and under the arms of the Penitente, naked above the waist, so that the cords cut through skin and into flesh, and every foot of progress through the sand was a torture. This also was an enactment of man's struggle against death.

The *Las Tinieblas*, or Earthquake, ceremony was similar to the Church *Tenebrae*, meaning "darkness, lower world, death" in Latin, and commemorated the flight of the apostles and the death of Christ, when darkness descended, rocks split, the earth shook, and the Temple veil was torn. It took place late on Good Friday night, was open to the public, and well attended by villagers and visitors of all ages.

All windows in the morada were covered, the door bolted, and one white candle and twelve yellow ones representing Christ and his disciples were lit. Wooden candelabra painted black might be used. A hymn preceded the reading of twelve psalms; one candle was extinguished after each. The *Rezador* hid the white candle, and pandemonium broke loose in the form of noise from instruments – pito, matracas, drums, rattling chains, beating on pots, accompanied by clapping, stamping, and screaming – to represent the earthquake following Christ's death. The Brothers whipped themselves for the last time in the back or in another room. Several minutes of *sudarios* for the dead, whose names were called out by the congregation, were interspersed. This continued for about an hour, then the white candle was brought forth, the others relit, and an *alabado* was sung. The villagers returned home, only Brothers remaining for the election and other business.

Lent customarily ended at noon on the Saturday of Glory; at night there was an exuberant dance to celebrate an end to privations. After this the Easter Sunday observances of solemn high mass and processions were rather anti-climactic, left largely to official Church supervision.

Death Ceremonies for the Penitentes

If a priest were available, rites of passage for a Catholic at death included the Last Sacrament, a wake, a requiem mass, burial in ground consecrated by the Church, and mourning, with a mass shortly after the funeral, and a memorial mass or novena one year after the death. Penitente ritual substituted an extended prayer service called a *rosario*, usually in the morada, for the Last Sacrament. Brothers took turns maintaining vigil during the *velorio de difunto* (wake for the dead) while the *Rezador* or *Cantador* chanted prayers and sang until dawn; the Brothers might form a flagellant procession, whipping themselves as they circled the body, thus assisting the journey of the dead Brother's soul. The body might only be taken to the morada for a brief service. Another *rosario* replaced the requiem mass, and the body of necessity could not always be buried in consecrated ground. *Rosarios* also took the place of memorial services. The Brothers charitably assisted non-Penitentes, those to whom the Church was unavailable, and poorer families unable to afford Church fees by contributing *rosarios, velorios*, and grave digging.

Religious Apparitions

The Penitentes also organized and maintained a communal society, fulfilling needs such as health care, welfare for the needy, and a judicial system. This followed the tradition of pious brotherhoods and trade guilds during the Middle Ages in Europe, which had become important religious-social-economic institutions. The trade guilds of Spain, developed only in the late twelfth century and operated according to ordinances issued by church, royal or municipal authority, at first were interrelated but grew apart as the trade guilds acquired political power, causing persecution and abolition, while the confraternities continued to be sanctioned.

In 1598 the Spanish had used printed images they had brought from Spain as visual aids to help explain the stories of the saints and the Passion of Christ to the native peoples; these evolved into carved and painted statues of the saints, called *santos*, made by Franciscan friars. During the Pueblo Revolt of 1680, most Christian imagery was destroyed. Local craftspersons and artists set up schools or *escuelitas*, and soon *santeros,* artists who made the images of saints, began to supply New Mexican churches, homes, and *moradas* with either two dimensional *(retablos)* or three dimensional *(bultos)* works. *Santeros* were usually paid for their work through trade or with livestock.

The wood of native trees, aspen and cottonwood root, were used for *bultos*, and pine for *retablo*, was used; water-based paints were made from local and traded vegetal and mineral pigments such as indigo, vermilion, clay, plants such as Chamisa and the cochineal insect from cactus.

The wood was primed with gypsum ground by hand, mixed with water and glue made from rabbit skins and animal hooves. After the painted image was finished, it was sealed with varnish made from pinesap.

The stories and images of the saints changed as word of mouth spread their stories; the isolation of the New Mexican villages made visits by priests rare occurrences. Individual Santos were prayed to in times of need: San Isidro, the patron saint of farmers, for a bountiful harvest; St. Barbara, patron of the home, to ward off dangers during thunderous lightning storms; St. Anthony to find husbands for unmarried girls and for fertility. Images of Our Lady of Solitude, Our Lady of Sorrows, and St. John of Nepomuk – a Bohemian priest martyred for keeping confidences and a symbol of secrecy – were popular. Since until the end of the eighteenth century Francis' order of Friars Minor had control in New Mexico, San Francisco de Asís is often depicted, wearing a monk's robe with cowl and knotted cord, bearded and tonsured, sometimes marked with stigmata on both hands. He may hold a cross and skull or a book, and is frequently pictured with animals. Figures representing Christ, some nearly life size, had articulated limbs so that they could be used as *Jesus Nazareno* or Man of Sorrows, Christ Crucified, and Christ in the Holy Sepulcher, though some *moradas* had different *bultos* for each. Village processions and celebrations centered around the treasured *santos* that were on display in the church and *morada* – in fact some *santos* no longer tolerated by the church were preserved by the Brothers. In the late 1700s, increasing numbers of religious images made in New Mexico took their place alongside imported pieces in churches and homes. These have been called the most powerful pieces of folk art to be found within the borders of the United States.

At least a dozen *santeros*, or saint-makers, were active in New Mexico by the 1820s and had developed a style grounded in the Spanish Catholic tradition and evolving art styles of Europe, distinctly New Mexican in character. The first native-born *santero* was Pedro Antonio Fresquis of Truchas, 1785-1831; he was followed by the Laguna Santero, Antonio Molleno, the Master of the Lattice-work Cross, and the Santero of the Mountain Village Crucifixes.

In the late 1800s, Juan Ramón Velásquez of Canjilón was one of the first *santeros* to use house paint, which was brought into the area after the arrival of the railroad. José Inés Herrera worked in El Rito from the late 1800s to the early 1900s, and was called the Death Cart Santero because of his large and threatening images. In the early and mid-1900s, Celso Gallegos carved unpainted figures and fulfilled the needs of the Agua Fria chapel in Santa Fe; José Dolores López was the first of a long line of unpainted aspen wood carvers in Córdova (his son George, who died in 1993, is known for his unpainted carvings of the Tree of Life).

Most *santos* were not signed, so that the artist is known only by his style. Many pieces are now in museums and private collections where they may be studied, and serve as inspiration for modern *santeros* such as Arthur Lopez, making traditional *bultos* based on his Roman Catholic religion, faithful representations of saints, but also through his *santos* giving cutting-edge social commentary. He has been receiving awards since he started carving full-time in 2000. Represented by Parks Gallery of Taos, his work appears in galleries in Washington, D.C., Scottsdale, Arizona, and in Chimayó; museums throughout the country collect his pieces.

A graphic designer with degrees in fine arts and design, Arthur Lopez had worked in Albuquerque and Los Angeles and was about to head to New York for a job with Macy's, when his father was diagnosed with cancer. He decided to stay in Santa Fe, and began painting again after his father's death, thinking of doing *retablos;* but, when he visited the Spanish market and saw the painted *bultos,* he realized that was what he wanted to do. He wanted his work to have substance, to be felt and not just seen.

Lopez uses old methods and materials, first drawing a two-dimensional sketch of the figure on a wood block, then carving. He boils rabbit-skin glue and adds either gypsum or marble dust to make gesso, which may be poured or painted on. For pigment, he tries to use natural colors, buying indigo from a wool-dying store, making cochineal red from a beetle, boiling black walnut shells for brown, using the mineral for yellow ochre. Gum Arabic acts as the binder.

Self Proclaimed Savior, *bulto* by Arthur Lopez

Varnish is made from the sap of piñon trees on his parents' property and put in a jar with grain alcohol. The piece is finished with a fine coat of beeswax.

A recent exhibit was titled *Con la Tinta de Mi Sangre* (With the Paint of my Blood), because Lopez says he slips and cuts himself at least once per piece. His art comes from his heart and his faith.

His work remains community-based. Lopez seeks out and collects the work of other *santeros*, and as a member and then chairman of the Spanish Colonial Arts Society Artist Liaison Committee, brings artists together at Christmas for a potluck dinner and gift exchange.

Chimayó

Back to **Chimayó**, the name meaning 'good flaking stone', i.e. obsidian. It had been established around an old Tewa pueblo after the reconquest in 1692; colonists were hard working, independent farmers and artisans who came to the area in hopes of receiving the title *hidalgo* (nobleman) if they stayed. They were frequently granted land, building lots, subsidies, and farming implements for the new life on the frontier. Chimayó was known for its weaving, an important industry, if only to make the necessary clothing in the early years. In 1805, inhabitants of Santa Fe had imported two fine weavers from Spain to help develop the craft; they soon moved to Chimayó, which became the capital of the weaving industry in the province. In 1900 commercial looms and yarns began to be used.

Oral tradition reports that during Holy Week on the night of Good Friday around 1810, Don Bernardo Abeyta, a Penitente, was performing penances around the hills of El Potrero when he saw a light bursting from a hillside near the Santa Cruz River. Digging barehanded, he found a crucifix, left it there and rushed to call the neighbors and the priest, Friar Sebastian Alvarez at Santa Cruz.

The six-foot cross bore the crucified image of *Nuestro Señor de Esquipales* – the Black Christ of Esquipales, Guatemala, over 2,000 miles from Chimayó. During the Spanish conquest of Central America, Mayan Indians in southeast Guatemala surrendered and agreed to accept the Catholic faith – yet they had endured so much cruelty from the Spaniards that they were deeply suspicious of a white Christ. A wood carver in the village of Esquipales was commissioned to carve a life-size *cristo* of brown wood; this was housed in a chapel built on the site of a Mayan shrine, near sulphurous springs. Incense burned at the altar gradually darkened the carving.

The crucifix was carried in a joyful procession back to the church and placed in the niche of the main altar. The next morning, it was gone, only to be found back in its hole. A second procession was organized and the Crucifix was returned to Santa Cruz, but once again it disappeared. This happened a third time, and everyone understood that *El Sefior de Esquipulas* wanted to remain in that place.

Some time later, Abeyta became ill, and one night feverishly stumbled to the chapel – he saw the Black Christ standing there, beckoning to him. Shedding his blanket, he staggered forward, but the apparition disappeared. When Abeyta knelt at the spot where it had been, he was instantly healed. Another legend claims that the vision beckoned him to a spot on the ground beneath the cottonwoods, where he was immediately cured.

Other miraculous cures began to take place. Pilgrims came.

Chimayó

When the Archbishop of Guatemala was cured of a contagious disease during a visit to the shrine, he ordered a sanctuary built on the spot. Abeyta had also written to Padre Alvarez, requesting permission to build a *sanctuario* on the site; the Vicar General of the diocese forwarded it to the Archbishop in Durango, Mexico, who granted permission. *El Santuario* (The Shrine) was built on the site between 1814 and 1816. The miraculous healings grew so numerous that the chapel had to be replaced by a larger Chimayó Shrine, an adobe mission, in 1816. It is in the style that had not changed substantially since the first churches of two hundred years earlier, with twin towers, a choir loft, *vigas*, a window over the altar, *retablos*, and a cemetery in front.

El Posito, the hole where the miraculous earth is obtained, was housed in a special candle-lit room behind the sacristy. The crucifix has almost been overshadowed by *El Posito*, the "sacred sand pit" from which it sprang. Crutches, braces, and messages of thanksgiving line the walls of small room. Healing sand is removed by the faithful and rubbed on the body in the hope of a cure.

Again, the soil of the place seemed to be an important factor in the healings; the people of Esquipales began manufacturing white tablets of the kaolin embossed with pictures of *El Cristo negro*, blessed by the local priests, and sold to pilgrims as a panacea. Such clay-eating has been a wide-spread phenomenon throughout history, practiced by both Mayans and the Indians of the American Southwest, but the village of Chimayó is the only place in the Southwest where pilgrimages of both Indians and Hispanics lead to a Catholic shrine to partake of *tierra bendita*, the blessed earth.

Between 1850-60, another miracle occurred – a villager driving cattle to his fields had his young daughter with him, and she heard a church bell ringing from beneath the ground. Soon he too could hear it, and they began to dig, unearthing a bell and under it, a wooden statue of the *Santo Niño de Atocha* (the Holy Child). The statue healed those who knelt before it. A private chapel to house it was built just west of the *Sanctuario*, and over the years the two rivaled each other in numbers of cures. Notes and photographs of those for whom special blessings are asked are pinned to the robes of this child Jesus. It is believed that the doll-like *Santo Niño* goes out of the chapel at night and wanders the countryside, listening to people's evening prayers and granting earnest requests; as a result of his nocturnal travel, his little shoes are scuffed and worn out, and people leave offerings of shoes.

Each year during Holy Week thousands of people make a pilgrimage to Chimayó to visit the *Santuario* and take away a bit of the sacred dirt. Pilgrims walk a few yards or a hundred miles. Many claim to have been cured there of diseases, infirmities, and unhappiness. The walls of the sacristy are hung with discarded crutches and before-and-after photographs as evidence of the healing. *El Santuario* was a privately owned chapel until the year 1929. At that time, several people from Santa Fe bought it and turned it over to the Archdiocese of Santa Fe.

La Llorona

The legend of **La Llorona** goes back to 1502, in the Aztec city of Tenochtitlan, where the goddess Cihuacoatl took the form of a beautiful lady draped in white garments. Throughout the night she cried out in misery, *"Oh hijos mios . . . ya ha llegado vuestra destruccion. Donde os llevare?"* (Oh my children...your destruction has arrived. Where can I take you?) Many believe that Cihuacoalt was speaking of the future conquest of Mexico by the Spaniards.

In 1505 a girl named La Malinche was born to a noble Aztec family in the province of Coatzacoalcos, and in 1515 given to Mayan merchants as a slave. In addition to her mother tongue of Nahuatl (Aztec), she learned to speak Mayan. In 1521 she gave birth to two twin boys by Cortés. The King and Queen of Spain, fearing that Cortés had betrayed them and was building his own empire, repeatedly asked him to return to Spain, but he refused, saying that if he left they would lose their new territories. They sent a beautiful Spanish lady to convince him to return. This lady seduced Cortés, convincing him to return to Spain with his two sons – Cortés told La Malinche of his decision to leave her behind. La Malinche, realizing that she had played a role in helping Cortés massacre her people, prayed to her gods for help;

one appeared to her and said, "If you let him take your children, one of them will return and destroy your people."

The night before Cortés' departure, La Malinche escaped with the babies. Cortés' soldiers soon discovered her absence and set out after her, surrounding her at the lake that Mexico City now rests on. She pulled out a dagger and stabbed her babies in the heart, dropping their lifeless bodies into the water with the heart-wrenching cry, "*Oh, hijos mios*." (Oh, my children.)

Up to the time of her death in 1531 she was seen and heard near the lake weeping and wailing for her children, and given the name 'La Llorona', the crying woman. Cortés left a letter preserved in the Spanish archives in which he wrote: "After God, we owe the conquest of New Spain to Doña Marina (La Malinche)." Thus in Mexico 'Malinche' became a word denoting betrayal.

The first documented appearances of La Llorona after La Malinche's death were in Mexico City in 1550; most often she is seen on the night of a full moon, wandering the streets wearing a white dress with a light veil covering her face, uttering agonizing cries. Her last stop is always La Plaza Mayor where she vanishes into the lake.

Adapted to the arroyos of New Mexico, a variation is that back in the days of the conquistadors, there lived a beautiful peasant-class woman named Maria. She married a wealthy, adoring husband who gave her everything she wanted. They had two boys, but soon after he lost interest in her, went out, and left her home alone. She saw him in a carriage with another woman while she was out taking the children on a stroll; enraged, she threw her children into the river, afterward starving herself to death and collapsing on the riverbank. Her spirit is often seen wandering by the river along the drainage ditch, searching for her lost children.

In the 1970s Bernadine Santistevan, growing up in a small northern New Mexico town, was told stories of La Llorona. Along with the other children, Bernadine was told that if she played by the river alone or misbehaved, La Llorona would take her away. She directed the film *The Cry* in 2003, a contemporary supernatural thriller that includes much of the factual discoveries about La Llorona that she came across in research.

La Llorona, *bulto* by Arthur Lopez

The city of Bernalillo still celebrates the Fiesta of San Lorenzo with its dance-drama *Los Matachines,* traced back to medieval Europe. The ritual tells the story of Montezuma, Cortez, and Malinche, who is portrayed by a young girl dressed in white, symbolizing a link between the Spanish and Mexican Indian forces.

The Virgin of Guadalupe

The first apparitions of **La Virgen de Guadalupe**, a Mexican icon that has become a most popular religious and cultural image, occur in Mexico in 1531, the year of La Malinche's death. She appeared to Juan Diego Cuauhtlatoatzin on the hill of Tepeyac near Mexico City from December 9 through December 12 speaking in Nahuatl, the language of the Aztecs. *La Virgen de Guadalupe* instructed him to build an abbey on the site. However, when Juan Diego spoke of this to the Spanish bishop, Fray Juan de Zumárraga, the prelate asked for a miraculous sign – so the Virgin told him to gather flowers from the hill, even though it was winter, when normally nothing bloomed. He found Spanish roses, bundled them in his *tilma*, and presented them to the bishop; an icon of the Virgin of Guadalupe remained imprinted on the cloth.

A number of historical documents support this account of the apparition, including a tract about the Virgin printed in 1649; a Spanish-language book about apparitions, *Imagen de la Virgen María* by Miguel Sanchez printed in 1648; a seventeenth-century engraving by Samuel Stradanus, which used the image to advertise indulgences; and the Codex Escalada, a pictographic account of the Virgin on Tepeyac, printed on deerskin, and said to date back to 1548.

The image is often seen as a code; Miguel Sanchez, author of the 1648 tract, described the Virgin's image as the Woman of the Apocalypse from the New Testament Revelation 12:1, "arrayed with the sun, and the moon under her feet, and upon her head a crown of twelve stars." Mateo de la Cruz argued twelve years later that the Guadalupe possessed all the iconographical attributes of Mary in her Immaculate Conception, and a 1738 sermon by Miguel Picazo argued that the Guadalupe was the "best representation" of the Immaculate Conception.

Many writers describe the image as containing coded messages for the indigenous people of Mexico. The Aztecs had an elaborate, coherent symbolic system for making sense of their lives – when this was destroyed by the Spaniards, something new was needed to fill the void and make sense of the new culture. Thus, this may have been Mary, mother of the Christian God, appearing in the guise of an Aztec female deity known as Tonantzin to the native population, fusing Christian religion with Native American beliefs. The name 'Guadalupe' may be a corruption of the Nahuatl name 'Coatlaxopeuh', which means 'Who Crushes the Serpent' – referring to Quetzalcoatl, one of the chief Aztec gods, whom the Virgin Mary 'crushed' by inspiring the conversion of indigenous people to Catholicism. The blue-green mantle of Guadalupe is in the color once reserved for the divine couple Ometecuhtli and Omecihuatl; her belt is read as a sign of pregnancy; and a cross-shaped image symbolizing the cosmos and called *nahui-ollin* is said to be inscribed beneath the image's sash. Guadalupe has also been seen as 'goddess of the maguey' and pulque was drunk on her feast day – a report in 1772 described the rays of light around Guadalupe as maguey spines.

The peasant who first saw her, Juan Diego Cuauhtlatoatzin, was canonized in 2001. Guadalupe's feast day is celebrated on December 12, and her image can be seen painted on the walls of houses in Martineztown and Barelos in Albuquerque. She is also represented in carved *santos,* standing in a body halo, supported on an upturned crescent and with a winged angel.

Mural with the Virgin of Guadalupe, 10th and Coal, Albuquerque

Painting doors of a house facing west "Virgin Mary blue" was protection against ghosts. When the body of a deceased was taken out of a house, it always had to be through one of the western doors. Mirrors were thought to be traps for the spirit, and thus were covered. All windows had to be opened to allow the spirit to leave. The link between clocks and life expectancy dates to the medieval period and was probably brought to New Mexico by the Spanish.

The Virgin of Guadalupe protects a house on Mountain Road, Albuquerque.

Divine Revelations: The Peyote Ceremony

The Mescalero Apache took their name from the mescal cactus (maquey or century plant), whose root crowns were used extensively for food – it supplied them with food, beverage and fiber. They had followed a hunting, gathering, and later raiding lifestyle, building brush shelters or erecting tepees. It was the custom to chop off the larger leaves and roots of twenty to thirty agaves during May or June, 'pressure cook' them in a rock-bottomed pit for hours, and to spread what was not eaten in thin sheets to be dried on flat rocks and taken home for storage. Dried mescal and mescal 'pudding' are still served at the coming of age ceremony for young women in early July.

The Mescalero Apache Indian Reservation was established by Executive Order of President Ulysses S. Grant in 1873, and is in the South Central part of New Mexico, in Otero County. Mescalero Indians numbered about 400 when their reservation was established, but the Lipan and Chirichua Apache were also placed there in the early 1900s, resulting in a population now exceeding 4,000.

In religious ceremonies, the Mescalero also utilize mescaline, a psychedelic drug derived from the small, spineless cactus Lophophora williamsii. Mescal is found in the Mexican Valley of the Rio Grande, the ancestral home of the Kiowa Indians, as well as in Texas; the peyote ritual became established first in the region of the Rio Grande in Texas where the cactus grows, and spread steadily among the Apaches, Omahas, Comanches, even used by tribes as far north as Wisconsin. The term peyote derives from the Nahuatl name *peyotl* for a cactus; the tops, called mescal buttons, which scarcely appear above ground, are dried and chewed, or added to alcoholic drinks. Mescaline is a crystalline alkaloid that has hallucinogenic effects and has been used in religious rites for over 3,000 years. It was used in Mexico in pre-Columbian times to induce supernatural visions and as a medicine.

As a part of the ghost dance, peyote use spread quickly among the Indian tribes of America after 1880. Indian prophets like Quanah Parker added Christianity to traditional beliefs and formed the basis of the peyote ritual still practiced today. Christian missionaries made an effort to prevent the Indians from obtaining the plant, resulting in prohibitions and legal actions, but Indians insisted that through it they were brought several steps nearer to heaven and that it helped them to lead better lives and to forsake alcoholic drinks.

James Mooney, a Smithsonian Institute archeologist, traveled through Oklahoma in 1891 to participate in peyote ceremonies; he became convinced of the need to unite the Indians, and protect their legal right to worship with peyote. He called together a conference in 1918, wrote the charter for and incorporated the Native American Church, which by the year 1922 claimed 22,000 members. The aims of the intertribal organization incorporated as The Native American Church of the United States are to foster and promote religious belief in God and the customs of the several tribes of Indians throughout the United States in the worship of a Heavenly Father, and to promote morality, sobriety, industry, charity, and right living, and cultivate a spirit of self-respect and brotherly love and union among the members of the several tribes of Indians throughout the United States, with and through the sacramental use of peyote. It claims that by eating peyote the Indian absorbs God's Spirit in the same way that Christians absorbs that spirit by means of the sacramental bread and wine.

The peyote religion was introduced to Taos Pueblo in 1907, but elders rejected the practices of the Native American Church as foreign to traditional pueblo beliefs, though some members nevertheless continued to participate.

Numerous efforts were made on State and Federal levels to outlaw peyote, laws banning it were enacted in eleven southwestern states; but in 1960 Arizona Judge Yale McFate ruled that the Native Americans were guaranteed use of peyote in religious ceremonies under first and fourteenth amendment rights. Nationally, the civil rights movement ushered in an era of social consciousness, and the time was ripe for reform in Indian affairs. In 1964, a landmark case was heard in California: on April 28, 1962, a group of Navajos had met in Needles to perform a religious ceremony including the use of peyote. They were arrested and tried for violating the law; Judge Mathew O. Tobriner of the California Supreme Court issued the court's decision, stating that Indian use of peyote was a religious freedom. Their right to do so has been continually reaffirmed. Aldous Huxley experimented with peyote in 1953, writing *The Doors of Perception*, which sparked mass interest and helped start the Psychedelic Revolution.

In San Luis Potosi, the sacred cactus is gathered in the fall, and those who do so work with the awareness of the sacred nature of their mission. For several weeks before the expedition starts, those who are to take part prepare with prayers and fasting, abstaining from sexual intercourse. The party proceeds accompanied by chanted prayers and sacred verses, with pack animals to bring back the harvest. Before reaching the holy place, members of the expedition perform a public penance. They then approach the plants, uncovering their heads, bowing to the ground, and burning copal incense; they may cross themselves in the manner of the Catholic Church. Discharging arrows to right and left of the plant to ward off evil spirits, they dig the cacti up with care and place them in jars. As the expedition returns, the villages through which it passes rejoice; peyote is offered on the altars and fragments given to every person met. An amount is stored for festivals, the rest is sold. The plant is cut into thick, fleshy slices laid in the sun to dry, becoming wrinkled brown discs covered with tufts of short white hairs, which in this form are known as 'mescal buttons'.

Many Indian tribes went off in isolation to contemplate and fast until a supernatural vision was achieved; this was now replaced by a collective all night vigil in which, through prayer, contemplation, and eating peyote, a divine revelation was received. Among Kiowa Indians, the peyote ritual generally takes place on a Saturday night; men sit on carefully swept earth in a circle about a fire. All pray, then the leader of the ceremony hands four buttons to each. Freed from the tufts of hair that cover it, the button is thoroughly softened in the mouth, ejected into the palm, rolled into a bolus, and swallowed. A many as twelve buttons may be taken at intervals between sunset and 3 a.m. with the accompaniment of occasional prayers and rites. Much of the time is spent in having each man, in rotation; sing four religious songs corresponding to hymns sung in churches. Throughout, the fire is kept burning brightly, and attendants maintain a continual beating of drums. The Indians remain seated from sundown to noon of the following day, and return to work without experiencing unpleasant aftereffects. As the effect wears off, they get up and go about their work; purely for ritual reasons, they abstain from using any salt with food on the following day.

Hispanic Influences

El Día de los Muertos

The Day of the Dead originated in Mexico, perhaps as long as 3000 years ago, has ancient Aztec and Mesoamerican roots, and is typically celebrated on November 1 (All Saints' Day) and November 2 (All Souls' Day). It is a joyful holiday with an emphasis on celebrating and honoring the lives of the deceased, and celebrating the continuation of life; the belief is not that death is the end, but the beginning of a new stage in life.

Since the 1980s, Albuquerque residents, particularly in the South Valley, have celebrated *Dia de los Muertos*, or day of the dead, to honor their ancestors. "[T]his is the time when you meet people," says Chuy Martinez, associate curator of education in the Cultural Services Department of the Albuquerque Museum. "You should be kind to everybody who is a complete stranger, because they may bring a message from your ancestors." A *velaciyn*, similar to a wake, highlights the event; this is a private ritual involving prayer, singing, and specific types of incense and flowers. Often *angelitos*, or young children who have died, are honored. A by-invitation-only ritual performed as it has been for thousands of years, the *velaciyn* is offensive to some churches and fundamentalists who consider it a pagan ritual.

The 'death cart' of the Penitentes may be incorporated into these observances. The tradition remembers that the Spanish entered with carts, and Doña Sebastiana, the patron saint of death, is represented as a skeleton figure with a bow and arrow. A shrub called *Yerba de la Flecha*, meaning 'the weed of the arrow', or the Sebastiana tree, grows in the mountains of Sonora and Sinaloa, Mexico. This shrub's name is derived from the past use of the mildly poisonous sap to coat arrows ('jumping beans' are the seed-pods of this shrub that contain the larva of a moth). People said prayers asking for another day to live. If this request was not to be granted, Doña Sebastiana would arrive at the house with her bow and arrow and shoot the person whose day it was to die. The making of such a cart for *El Día de los Muertos* can offer cultural identity; or can be done as a work of art.

Modern art depicting Doña Sebastiana for the Day of the Dead

Albuquerque families visit cemeteries where their loved ones are buried, clean and decorate the graves with *ofrendas*, or offerings, which often include orange marigolds called *'cempasuchil'* (*cempaxochitl), Nahuatl* for 'twenty flowers'. In modern times, the term *'Flor de Muerto'*, Spanish for 'Flower of the Dead', often replaces it. The flowers are thought to attract souls of the dead to the offerings. Toys are brought for dead children, and bottles of tequila, mezcal, pulque or atole for adults; the deceased's favorite candies and trinkets are also offered on the grave. *Ofrendas* are also installed in homes, usually with *pan de muerto* ('bread of the dead') and sugar skulls – in the post-Hispanic era, it was common to keep skulls as trophies and display them during the rituals to symbolize death and rebirth. Some believe the spirits of the dead eat the 'spiritual essence' of *ofrenda* food, so even though the food is eaten after the festivity, it lacks nutritional value. Pillows and blankets may be put out so that the deceased can rest after their long journey. These altars or small shrines usually have the Christian cross, statues or pictures of the Blessed Virgin Mary, pictures of deceased relatives and other persons, and many candles. Families spend time around the altar praying and telling anecdotes about the deceased. In some locations, celebrants wear shells on their clothing so when they dance the dead will wake up because of the noise. Some individuals dress up as the deceased.

The Penitentes marked All Saints' and All Souls' Day on November 1st and 2nd, and Indians also had a feast of the dead in conjunction with All Soul's Day. Bowls lined with upright ears of corn and the favorite foods of the dead were taken to marked graves in the churchyard, candles set and lighted around the periphery, by Isleta Pueblo Indians in the 1880s.

In Isleta Pueblo in about 1915, after the corpse had been washed and ritually prepared for the journey to the afterworld, it was laid out on a house ladder and carried first to church, then to the graveyard. The body was wrapped in a black *manta* and buried with the head to the south, a ritually 'killed' (broken) bowl placed on the grave. A hole containing food for the underworld, personal ceremonial gear, and other belongings and objects were traditionally placed some distance away.

In Santa Domingo Pueblo, located on the bank of the Rio Grande thirty to thirty-five miles southwest of Santa Fe, in the 1960s, stillborn babies were buried under the floor of the mother's house; males were buried to the north of the church, or left when facing the altar, in the cemetery, females buried to the south.

Descansos

Roadside shrines mark the spot where a fatal motor-vehicle accident or act of violence took place. Many victims died at the scene; others died later in hospitals. In the Southwest, these were originally *Descansos* (resting places), erected at places where a funeral procession paused to rest on the journey between the church and the cemetery, at a time when the coffin was shoulder by four or six men. An association was thus created between the road, the interrupted journey, and death as a destination. There was time for contemplation; perhaps someone would break off a sprig of juniper and bury it in the ground to mark the spot, or place wild flowers there along with a cross. Plastic floral decorations are often used. "Anyone who's traveled in Mexico and Central America has seen these ... When I was in Honduras, we were warned on the Day of the Dead to be careful driving because people would be out putting flowers on the crosses," said Father Joe Anderson, pastor of Holy Family Catholic Church in Deming. "These shrines are a commemoration for the families and to remind others to drive carefully and pray for those who died. The Catholic Church doesn't require them; the people put them up of their own devotion," Anderson said.

Penitentes would erect small piles of stones, sometimes surmounted with a small wooden cross or a carved stone marker, to mark places where the procession of mourners carrying a coffin to the cemetery had stopped to sing hymns, called *alabados*. Believers stopped at these *descansos* to say a prayer for the dead and perhaps place another stone on the pile.

The Penitentes of Cuba, New Mexico, made a pilgrimage on foot lasting several weeks called the *Procesión del Estandarte* to San Ysidro, where there was a ceremony in the morada, to Marquez (then known as Juan Tafoya), to Moquino, to Cubero, and on to St. John's, Arizona. On the return trip they may have stopped at San Mateo and Cabezon. The Procession of the Standard stopped to worship at a descanso and cross beside the road between the settlement of Piedra Lumbre and Moquino, which marked the resting place for funeral processions walking to the cemetery at Moquino or Cebolleta. The practice was discontinued about 1912.

Descanso at curve of the road near Madrid

Brujas and Curanderas

New Mexico's first witches had a long journey from Spain to colonial Mexico, then up the long oxcart trail called the Jornad del Muerto, bringing wisdom and mystic powers that had taken centuries to develop. They both cured and caused illness; foretold the future; and had supernatural powers. Evil witches were called *brujas*, and good ones *curanderas*, or *curanderos* in the case of men, in New Mexican folklore. Curanderas used mystical powers, native herbs, and potent substances to heal and alleviate suffering – they played an important role in early New Mexico, curing physical ailments and relieving mental distress. They are still respected; the State Coverage Insurance (SCI) provides for 'traditional medicine benefits and services performed by a curandero or curandera'. Brujas, using their powers for sinister purposes, knew about human greed, could use 'the evil eye', knew how to win a lover's devotion or destroy a rival.

New Mexico's witches are said to ride fireballs, not brooms, and can clutch a pumpkin, gourd, or even an egg in order to levitate. They can also turn into owls. Residents have seen luminous globes flitting between trees, or watched balls of light bounce over a suspected witch's home.

San Luis is overlooked by Cabezon Peak, which is sacred to Indians: the volcanic peak is called 'the Giant's Head' from a story of the Twin War Brothers killing a giant on what is now Mt. Taylor. His spilled blood is supposed to have created the lava beds at Grants, and his head rolled to rest forty miles east. The peak, called Tse Najiin (black rock) by the Navajo, traditionally marked the eastern boundary of Navajo territory. The town of Cabezon, five miles north of the peak, was first settled in 1826 by Juan Maestas, who called it *La Posta*, 'the stage stop', as it served as an important way station on the stagecoach route from Santa Fe to Fort Wingate. In its prime it contained houses, saloons, dance halls, and general stores on both sides of the Rio Puerco; due to frequent flooding caused by the river, buildings were later moved up and away from it. The name was changed to Cabezon in 1891, but it was all but abandoned by the 1940s.

In San Luis mischievous fireballs were said to have chased people down by the river and to have bounced along treetops, leaving them unscorched. A boy riding a mule wagon past an empty house there suddenly had to contend with 'a terrible ball of fire' shooting out and rolling beneath the mules, who lit out running with the boy in tow and the fireball still entangled in their legs. Neighbors investigated the house, which showed no sign of life, but when they left they saw 'sparks of fire' coming from the chimney.

Also in San Luis, a hitchhiker mysteriously vanished from his seat beside the driver. A man chased a coyote into an arroyo to find the animal transformed to a Navajo woman in a shawl. A late night traveler encountered a dark spirit on the road, which crossed in front of him and disappeared into the sagebrush.

In Albuquerque, **Casa de Ruiz**, built around 1706, was a residence for the Ruiz family until the last inhabitant, Rufina G. Ruiz, died in 1991 at the age of ninety-one. The house is built of *terrones*, a type of adobe brick used when the area around the Rio Grande River was a marshy swamp. After the drainage system for the swamp was installed around 1820, adobe bricks were made with a dryer mud as they are today. The walls are in places over two feet thick, to keep the house warmer in the winter season and cooler in the summer months.

The Sanborn maps, first used in 1891 by the Sanborn Insurance Company to estimate property values and claims and now located at the University of New Mexico Engineering Library, show the Ruiz house as it was before 1900. It was built in the classic Old Spanish 'U-shape' hacienda style and remained so with only minor changes until 1920, when a flood destroyed half of the house. The house is shown as being on School Street, now Church Street, across from the San Felipe de Neri Church. Originally the back parking lot of the church was Old Town Plaza, and the current convent was a Catholic school, resulting in the name School Street from the early 1700s to the late 1800s.

The Ruiz family can be traced back to Julianna Lucero and Francisco Ruiz, both born around 1834. No record of their ancestors has been found, but the dwelling might have been several generations old by this time. Their daughter, Sarah Ruiz, born on February 22, 1880, was a passionate woman who had many love affairs, though she never married; she was also a curandera. Rufina was her daughter.

The new owner, Marie Coleman, felt distinct resistance as she began remodeling for the Church Street Café, even clearly hearing a female voice shout at her to get the contractor out of the building. She later learned that the contractor was actually the grandson of one of Sarah Ruiz's love affairs that did not end well.

The next man to work on the house complained that a woman was kicking buckets around; Marie simply asked her to stop, explaining that she was trying to fix up her house, and she did. After that Marie would speak to her presence – which sought attention by throwing pebbles, levitating and smashing coffee cups, stealing keys, etc. Church Street Café, where staff still see Sarah materialize upon occasion, is at 2111 Church NW.

Church Street Cafe

Ghost Towns

Leading an expedition in search of the legendary Seven Cities of Gold, Coronado pressed as far as Kansas before giving up; having seen the great mineral wealth produced by Mexico's northern provinces, the thinking was that New Mexico would yield gold as well. But there was no mining in New Mexico before the Spanish arrived. Natives only prospected riverbeds and canyons for pottery clay and mined hillsides for building stones. Don Juan de Oñate called salt 'one of the four riches of New Mexico', but the others failed to materialize.

The natives did trade in turquoise, prized for its ornamental and ceremonial value – beads found at Chaco Canyon indicate that these mines, at Cerrillos, date back at least a thousand years. The pueblo of Acoma gave turquoise to Coronado's army.

For Indians, turquoise had a relationship to bringing rain; it was said to be found by going to the end of a rainbow after a storm and digging in the damp earth. A bead of turquoise affixed to a gun or bow made it shoot accurately. For the Navajo, a turquoise bead had protective powers. Turquoise was the Apache medicine man's badge of office; among Mexicans it was the distinguishing mark or badge of priesthood.

Mexicans adorned idols with it, and buried it with the dead, saying it was the dead man's heart. They were also accustomed to say that at one time men had been stones, at last they would return to stones, and a small green stone interred with the bones of the dead stood for the principle of life. One of the myths of the birth of Quetzalcoatl describes his mother, while sweeping, finding turquoise and swallowing it, which resulted in her pregnancy.

There were veins of silver within Chalichihuitl Mountain in Cerrillos, and the Spaniards used slave labor from Tano Pueblo to excavate it: a cave-in here may have fueled the Pueblo Revolt, after which the mine was filled and obliterated, lying dormant for 150 years.

Madrid

In 1828 a cache of gold was found in the Ortiz Mountains between Golden and Madrid, marking it as the oldest gold-mining district in the U.S., but it was not developed until the 1860s, when the rush for gold in California and Colorado spilled into New Mexico. In 1879, the gold, silver, and turquoise of Cerrillos were rediscovered, leading to a rush to the area – copper, lead, and zinc were also present. The problem was lack of water, without which mining on any kind of scale could not be done; Thomas Alva Edison spent over two million dollars at a laboratory in the Ortiz Mountains endeavoring to separate gold from rock through an electrostatic process rather than by the use of water. By 1880 there were fifty-five mines producing mostly silver, but some gold – and a million dollars' worth of turquoise. The town boomed until 1900, when the mineral-filled hills were spent and mines began shutting down.

Coal ash in ruins even older than Chaco shows that coal was mined in New Mexico as long as 12,000 years ago. In **Madrid**, a thriving coal-mining town of 3,000 in the early 1900s, unlimited electricity had become available by the 1920s, and this spawned dramatic Christmas light displays that even drew national airlines to alter night routes to offer views.

The town shrank to thirteen after Los Alamos, the last buyer of its coal, switched to gas in 1959 – the Christmas lights went out in the early 1940s, with a brief respite during WW II when the coal town of Madrid fueled the atomic city of Los Alamos. The original Christmas lights were eventually sold to Gallup.

Madrid

Madrid has become an artsy tourist stop since the seventies, when artists, gallery owners, and people seeking an alternative lifestyle bought abandoned mining shacks at attractive prices; the tradition of Christmas light displays began again and still continues.

The Mine Shaft Tavern was the last of the company town buildings erected in 1946; its 40-foot lodge pine bar is the longest stand-up bar in New Mexico, and most furnishings are the original ones. The house beer was called Dead Canary Ale, made by Santa Fe Brewing in what was formerly a motorcycle restoration shop. On weekends, to date, bikers ride out and park their motorcycles in front of the tavern, and there's live music.

Mineshaft Tavern, Madrid

Glasses have been seen to fly off the bar and break; doors are also known to open and swing back and forth on their own. Objects are moved around after hours, and sounds come from the adobe walls, especially in the small room on the north side. Brief sightings of ghosts have been reflected in mirrors. There is a 'restroom ghost', female, both seen and heard, who sometimes wanders into the kitchen and breaks dishes or flicks lights on and off in the bar. Some believe that the ghost is of a young woman who was killed in an automobile accident directly in front of the tavern.

La Ventana

South of the old coal mining town of La Ventana is one of the largest land grants in New Mexico, given to the Cabeza de Vaca family, descendents of the Spanish explorer, in 1815. It consisted of more than one hundred thirteen thousand acres, containing the **Ojo del Espirito Santo** (Holy Ghost Spring). The name is said to come from the experience of a man standing guard one night after dinner, who rushed to camp crying "El Espirito Santo! El Espirito Santo!" The campers went with him to see two wraithlike spirals rising from the ground in the nearby canyon, seeming to them to be a manifestation of the Holy Ghost. Following the spirals to discover the spring, they named it after the apparition. The estate was sold to the Jemez Tribe in 1933, which runs a recreation area at the site of the Holy Ghost Springs.

According to legend, a small party of Spaniards in the 1540s, pursued by Indians, took shelter at the base of **Magdalena Peak**. On the east slope, they saw a woman's face outlined in rocks and shrubs, reminding them of a similar mountain in Spain where, following the death of Mary Magdalene, her face appeared miraculously carved into the stone. The belief was that Magdalena Peak offered white men protection from the Indians. The peak must have had significance to the Apaches, because miners working the slopes were never attacked.

Magdalena

The town of Magdalena prospered from its beginnings in 1884 because the Santa Fe Railroad completed a branch line from Socorro to there in order to ship ore from the Kelly mines, two miles up the mountain, to the smelter at Socorro. This was also used as a stockyard railroad, with cattle herders making the drive to Magdalena on what became known as the Beefsteak Trail. Cowboys sometimes brought in as many as 100,000 head of sheep and cattle – and then patronized the saloons and brothels. In 1897, Magdalena also began shipping wool to eastern markets. But in 1929, the Bank of Magdalena failed, and in the 1930s a saturated cattle market and drought, plus a government-established wool warehouse in Albuquerque, finished the town off. In 1972, the railroad abandoned the branch line, and by then fires had destroyed eighty percent of the old business district.

Colfax

Colfax, situated close to other towns on two railroads in the heart of rich farming land, with nearby mountains abounding in wild game for the hunter, should have been successful, but only stayed alive for about twenty-five years from 1908 to 1933. The Great Depression of 1929 sealed its fate when gasoline prices forced people to give up driving, and most moved to nearby larger towns such as Dawson, Raton, Springer, and Cimarron.

The Weeping Lady of Colfax is the apparition of a woman who appears in the back row of the combination church and schoolhouse here – worshippers have thought that she was a normal mourning church visitant until she vanished. She is the spirit of a mother still grieving for her young son, who died of an unknown illness in the late 1800s; inconsolable grief killed her within a few months of her son's death. Reported phenomena include sounds of sobbing, the cries of a young boy, and disembodied footsteps have been heard in the church/schoolhouse. At times the mother appeared as a ball of light that floated and wandered through the abandoned town. A scent of roses and feelings of profound sadness are brought by the ghost.

An apparition of a woman, haggard in appearance and wearing a long grey dress, has also been spotted around the ruins of the town and seen by motorists, walking north along the freeway. She appears solid and is often mistaken as a hitchhiker by passing motorists, but when they pull over to offer assistance, she has already vanished. There are also two reports of 'glowing balls of light' that have been seen moving about the ruins when the moon is full.

Mountainair

Mountainair's **Schaffer Hotel** was built in 1923 by eccentric Clem 'Pop' Shaffer, and he still haunts the east wing. Clem and his wife Pearl arrived in Mountainair in 1908; they eked out a meager living until Pearl's death in 1911. He then married Lena 'Mom' Shaffer, with the help of whose wealthy father the couple turned the hotel into a thriving business. They had a rollicking, boisterous relationship, and Pop became well known as a heavy drinker, carouser, and ladies' man – Mom used to lock him up during his binges, and there's a bullet hole in the pressed-tin ceiling in the lobby by the stairs where she took a pot shot at him and missed.

Pop lovingly decorated the Shaffer with paintings, found-wood carvings, and a fanciful stone and cement fence outside the garden. The structure of this derived from the blacksmith shop that had originally been the purpose of the building; Pop kept burning it down accidentally, and had created poured concrete walls reinforced with iron auto parts to keep this from happening.

Its heyday was in the 1930s. The structure's style is often called Pueblo-Deco, but really it was the unique creation of the distinctive hand of Pop, who painted the ceiling of the hotel's flourishing restaurant with colorful Native American-based designs.

Painted ceiling at the Schaffer Hotel, Mountainair

Painted ceiling at the Schaffer Hotel, Mountainair

Albuquerque native Joel Marks ate in what was then the café in 2003, fell in love with the place and bought it, hiring as live-in innkeepers John and Karen Cate. Nineteen rooms were beautifully refurbished; it was noticed that there was a definite energy in the place, especially in the east wing, which is over the painted ceiling of the restaurant. At night banging objects were heard, people talking, laughing, and arguing. While the Cates were the only ones in the hotel, they said the ghost would play with the elevator, opening and closing doors. Water fountains would spring to life, and once during a local get-together, people heard water running upstairs – in a locked room to which the key hadn't yet been found. A boy was boosted through the transom to open the door, and the bathtub inside was running, its faucet handle mysteriously turned.

Today the hotel, at 103 West Main Street, forms an integral part of the small arts community of Mountainair. It is on the National Register of Historic Places.

Following Obsessions: The Fabulous Treasures of the Gypsy

Pamela Armas, a fabric designer who has set up cottage industries to produce her work in India, Nepal, and Pakistan, has collected motifs and textile work from all over the world. Originally from San Diego, eight years ago, Armas says, "I was driving the trade show truck down the road through Mountainair and something drew me to turn back. I think I could live here," I said to my friend, and she told me, "I haven't seen you in anything but three and a half inch heels and a dress for years, are you crazy?" But this is the closest she could come to living in the Rajasthan Desert, Armas says – she returned home and showed her husband photos of the building, saying, "I've made an investment!" A contractor, he looked at the dilapidated property and said, "I think you've just lost money!"

Ornamental art gates now shine at the doors of the double storefront on the main street. The room on the left holds wares for the twenty trade shows Armas does a year; shelves she had made in Thailand hold fabric of silk, gold-threaded, shimmering organza plus the beads, tassels, and two dozen or more little shoes for dolls – made in Mexico and India.

Walls inside are painted in rich reds and oranges, and some rooms are decorated and named in honor of the energy generated by individuals. In the Gypsy Tea Room, her sister Lise Peeples created her first wall painting including the three Gypsy sisters entwined in dance, Pamela's bichon Chibi, the most benevolent moon, up in a corner. Next is the Frida Kahlo Room, her sister's second wall painting, containing the detailed accuracy of Frida's paintings, yet also with ethereal qualities. The *ofrenda* is lined with dolls, and there's a Frida Kahlo chair. On the table in its hand sewn box is a visual journal, the Frida Kahlo Book, its pages appliqued, beaded, sequined, and French-knotted, imprinted with photographs – a lavish and loving record of Pamela's obsession with the artist. This was a communal work, as was the *Gypsy Book*. "Sometimes I just have to go sit in the Frida Kahlo room," Armas says, expressing her feelings of connection with and deriving reinforcement from Frida Kahlo's spirit.

Sculptures of boiled wool are atop a table outside the 'office', where there's a countertop of dolls of ingenious imagining, one with quill feathers encrusted with gold. Faces made in Europe have a wry, humorous cast. Soft sculptures include a marvelous long lizard, and a Frog Prince: "Oh that's the work of the polyester pantsuit lady," Pamela says, and explains that she and her friends would send those to her and she would sculpt and stuff and paint them. The Chinese bed in Zhang Yimou's film *Raise the Red Lanterns* was rented from Armas, and there are exquisite carved chairs and painted cabinets throughout. The private living area has muted light, the traditional perforated tin lamps of New Mexico, luxurious throws, and hangings.

Pamela Armas plans to start up an annual artist's retreat here as soon as the town can support it. There's enough accommodation in 2008, but not enough provision for feeding forty to fifty participants. In fact, when I was there, a group of people wandered down Main Street looking for a place to have a latte – and there wasn't one! But Pamela doesn't want to change the ambiance of the peaceful town.

Working with lavish fabrics and trim, expression will be given through visual journaling, art quilting, and doll-making to the passions, inner fixations, and dreams of the artist.

Expressing Rich Hispanic Home-town Roots

Exit 240 leads to Bernalillo, where Tim Lucero and Zenon Cruz, partners in Project 240 Apparel were born and raised; they've known each other since they were kids, and married sisters. Tim has a B.A. in Advertising Art and is a graphic designer; Zenon is an entrepreneur in construction who has a great deal of business experience that he uses creatively for the partnership.

T-shirts designed by Project 240 are cultural statements that express identity – catch phrases that are an amalgam of personal experiences, culture, and art, reflecting lifestyle and traditions. "El Chupacabra made me do it" refers to the Hispanic version of Bigfoot, a legendary animal that goes around farms at night and sucks the blood out of goats. Tim had never heard of it until he saw an episode of the 'X Files'. Early on in a brainstorming session they came up with the idea of putting 'Big Daddy Huevos' – the name of a real bull in Bernalillo – across a T-shirt; 'Chingon' is another bestseller. Then there's 'Champions Eat Frijoles' and 'Soy Macho' ... with a little rebellion attached: rappers Malverde and Bajaras have worn Project 240 T-shirts. The target market for these cool, hip, funny T-shirts is the young urban Hispanics age sixteen to thirty-five.

Tim and Zenon are proud of coming from a little town in the desert – and are involved with the school system and community, also assisting a charity called Project New Day that helps homeless children; they participate in the fashion show and silent auction. Zenon was raised in government housing, on the rough side of town. Tim was raised right in the heart of Bernalillo. Tim has known his wife since they were eleven or twelve; she encouraged him to pursue a career in art, and he also has had a lot of family support. He says he was always around religious art and Hispanic art; a friend's father, Filimon Aguilar, taught him to carve *santos*, but that's a project that is on the back burner now. He is delighted to be working for the top advertising agency in the region, Vaughn Wedeen Creative.

Sports New Mexico carries Keith Jardine shirts. Project 240 created for Si-TV, the Latino cable network, a wardrobe for hosts, guests, and the audience, and has been asked to do it again. Business has been mostly through the Internet thus far, but the partners are in the process of negotiation with boutiques and shops, and anticipate being in ten stores nationwide shortly. Designs have gone from witty humor to work with a deeper concept, more artistic – one of the latest reads "*a pura fuerza*," full force, or "with everything you got" – and that's the idea behind the whole company.

Church of San Felipe de Neri, Old Town

The Founding of Albuquerque

Albuquerque was home to several groups of Native American peoples as far back as the ice age 25,000 years ago, and continues to be a center of Native American culture. Spanish colonists attracted to the banks of the Rio Grande by green pastures on which to graze sheep founded Albuquerque as a villa in 1706. The first structure built was a church named for the city's patron saint, San Felipe de Neri.

In petitioning the Spanish government for permission to establish a city, provisional governor of the territory Don Francisco Cuervo y Valdez suggested to the Duke of Alburquerque, responsible for preliminary approval of the application, naming it after him; the first 'r' in the original name was later dropped.

In the mid-1800s, Anglo settlers were bringing a new government and a dominant culture which was not exclusively Catholic or even Spanish-speaking. Initially, the Penitentes helped in the adjustment period. Later in the century, the Catholic Church took the viewpoint that the Penitentes were contrary to modern ecclesiastical order and harmful to the image of Catholicism in the eyes of newcomers from the East; they were to be forced to 'return' to the Third Order of St. Francis. Flagellation and cross carrying in public were forbidden. The art of the *santeros* also suffered as traders and merchants began to introduce commercially produced plaster of Paris statues, slowly replacing the need for their craft, which was considered crude and primitive in the eyes of the French priests newly assigned to the region in the 1860s. Church authorities repeatedly tried to suppress the society or regulate its actions. Archbishop Salpointe issued a stringent order on the subject on March 31, 1889.

Mural on the wall of La Hacienda restaurant in Old Town, telling the history of the establishment of the Villa de Albuquerque in the early eighteenth century.

Always secretive, the Penitentes went further underground. But they now had to function under a government in which church and state were separate; this caused the enactment of a series of laws incorporating Brotherhoods as benevolent societies with legal rights. Becoming incorporated, nonprofit benevolent associations, they acquired both political and judicial expertise, though they had a hard time adjusting to the jury system, having sworn to protect fellow members and to abide by the decisions of their officers. Moradas provided blocs of votes, easily influenced if the politician underwent a mild initiation and token self-punishment. They fulfilled some of the need for adequate Spanish-American representation.

During the nineteenth century, Albuquerque served as purveyor of goods to the West as a link in trade with Mexico. A trade and transportation center and important station on the Old Chihuahua Trail, it was an extension of the Santa Fe Trail. Many forts were established between 1850 and 1875 to protect westward immigration. Merchandise companies established warehouses and stores in Albuquerque. It never went through the wild days of the raw frontier as western towns did in the last quarter of the nineteenth century; there was already an established culture, a century and a half old. It became a U.S. Army post in 1846 and was occupied by the Confederacy for two months during the Civil War. In 1891 it was incorporated as a city.

It is said that an old man used to live in the caves at the top of **Haunted Hill**, located at the end of Menaul in the foothills, where he lured prostitutes and killed them. Some have reported an apparition of an old man coming after them, and a lantern swinging with no one carrying it has been spotted – one can hear screaming, footsteps, and bodies being dragged.

New Albuquerque started out as a train depot built in 1880 by the Atchison Topeka and Santa Fe Railroad; frame buildings housing a warehouse, restaurant, and hotel soon sprang up nearby. Corruption, scandal, and lawlessness plagued it, bringing the need for law and order. The first town marshal, Milt Yarberry, was a bad choice with a shady past, rumored to have been involved in several rustling and shooting scrapes on the Texas-Arkansas border. He had run a saloon and billiards hall in Texas and a dance hall in the town of Bernalillo.

In addition to being the first town marshal, he was first to be indicted for murder. On March 27, 1881, Yarberry gunned down a loud-mouthed, well-connected man, Harry Brown, at a restaurant at 2nd Street and Railroad Avenue (now Central Street), because he was a rival for the attentions of a beautiful local widow. Yarberry fired four shots; two or three shots after Brown was down. At the trial, Yarberry was acquitted after witnesses testified that Brown had threatened to kill him on sight.

Less than three months later, Yarberry killed Charles D. Campbell, a railroad carpenter, shooting him three times in the back – supposedly Yarberry and a gambler named Frank Boyd were investigating a shot fired in or near a restaurant on 1st Street south of Railroad Avenue, but the pistol Campbell allegedly fired when Yarberry demanded he "hold up [his] hands" was never found.

Yarberry was arrested but did not go to trial until May 1882; after deliberating only an hour, the jury found him guilty, and he was sentenced to be hanged.

Yarberry's lawyer appealed the verdict – and Yarberry escaped on September 9, 1882, but was caught a few days later at Arroyo Galisteo. He was returned by train for his execution on February 9, 1883, at Bernalillo County Jail, just east of the Plaza in Old Town. The first town marshal was buried in Santa Barbara Cemetery with the hanging rope still around his neck.

Cemeteries

In America, often the route to the cemetery was not the most direct one, because it was believed that spirits were attracted to the path of mourning; likewise, the Chinese have zigzag bridges so that ghosts can't follow. On the other hand, early settlers believed the same route could be used over and over in order to confine the spirits to one known location. The same superstition applied to known places of death, such as hanging trees – children were told ghost stories in an attempt to keep them away from such places.

It was also believed that ghosts could not see the color black; therefore black-garbed funeral attendees would not be followed back home by a ghost. Black veils served the same purpose when worn by women, to conceal their identities from ghosts. And if a woman was buried in black, she would return to haunt the family ...

My grandmother was a Seventh Day Adventist, and she told me as a child never to pluck flowers or leaves from trees, or their nuts, in a cemetery: I could take only what had fallen. There was a superstition that when passing a graveyard, one should turn pockets inside out to avoid bringing home a ghost in a pocket. Some believed that the safe way to get past a graveyard was to pick up a stone and carry it in the right hand until the boundary had been passed, then set it down and go on without looking back.

Santa Barbara Cemetery, which held graves dating back to 1870, was added onto with eighteen acres north of the original portion to form a new cemetery, Mount Calvary, in 1936. The shadowy apparition of a man wearing a hat and suit, holding a tattered rope attached to a noose about its neck, moves about the old section of the cemetery late at night when the moon is full – Yarberry, who gave a fifteen minute speech as his "last words," does not want to leave the living.

Dawson, New Mexico, named for John B. Dawson, a rancher who bought the coal-rich property from the Maxwell Land Grant in 1869, was incorporated by the Dawson Fuel Company in 1901, and sold to the Phelps-Dodge Company in 1906. Phelps-Dodge soon developed Dawson into a major coal source for the Southern Pacific and the Santa Fe railroads, laying down a model for the company town that was among the most progressive in New Mexico. Within years, downtown boasted a gym, an opera house, a movie theater, several schools, two churches, a large mercantile store, and a modern hospital, and the town had become the largest single-industry town in the Southwest.

On October 22, 1913, Stag Canyon Mine No. 2 was shaken by an explosion felt two miles away in the town proper. Relief teams rushed in, but of the 286 men who reported to work in the mine that morning, only twenty-three survived. Two rescuers also died during the rescue effort in the second worst mine disaster of the century. It was determined that the explosion had been caused by a dynamite charge igniting coal dust in the mine – a flagrant violation of mining safety laws. Mass funerals were conducted for the victims, row upon row of graves dug necessitating the extension of the cemetery far up the hill. The markers were white iron crosses, and burials continued for weeks.

Dawson continued as a successful mining town until, on February 8, 1923, Stag Canyon Mine No. 1 suffered an explosion when a mine cart jumped its tracks and ignited coal dust in the mine. There were 123 men in the mine; all but two, who had been in an isolated section of the mine, were killed, many of them children of the men who had died in 1913. The cemetery had to be extended once again.

However, Dawson did not become a ghost town until 1950, when the Phelps Dodge Corporation shut down the mine and the entire town was sold or razed. Today the only remaining landmark is the Dawson cemetery, with over 350 white iron crosses marking the graves of men who died in the mines. Over the years there have been several reports of 'ghost lights', round floating or bouncing auras of light, in the cemetery, appearing at the top of the hill near the cemetery and coming down into the graveyard. According to local legend, the lights issue from the lamps in the miners' helmets.

Numerous sightings of apparitions have been reported in the cemetery at night, seen at a distance and described as being mist-like and transparent.

In Albuquerque in 1892, the B'nai B'rith lodge incorporated the Jewish Cemetery Association and acquired two acres of land in what is now the Fairview Cemetery. The oldest part, called **Yale Cemetery** after the street that runs by it, contains the graves of veterans of the Spanish American War as well as many of New Mexico's former politicians. There are many upright tombstones typical of Victorian times, as well as ground level markers, and the large, mausoleum-like graves of governors and mayors. There are also the nameless dead, unidentified and/or unclaimed bodies, whose hundreds of graves are pushed off into the corners of the cemetery in dirt ground, pockmarked with the occasional beer bottle or a hole where a prairie dog has dug up their bones. Several personages dressed in old-fashioned clothing have materialized there at night. In 1902, Congregation Albert acquired what had been the Congregation Albert Cemetery for over one hundred years.

Into the Modern Day

The Penitentes continue to exist in New Mexico as a very hidden society. The Church saw them as problematical, though as early as 1853 a Penitente book of rules was approved by Bishop John Baptiste Lamy of the Diocese of Santa Fe. This book contained duties of officials as well as prayers. Rules for the Penitentes were officially approved by Bishop Lamy in 1856 (REF: Archives of the Archdiocese of Santa Fe LDD 1853 #17 and 1856 #11).

The moradas had served as the repositories of the village *santos*, from which they had been carried on special occasions and at times of illness or mourning; in the sixties these were regarded as garish, and were destroyed or plundered by outsiders. In the 1880s and 1890s, reformed rules were approved by succeeding Archbishops Salpointe and Bourgade (Archives of the Archdiocese of Santa Fe LDD [1886 #8], 1891 #6, and 1899 #8), but the Penitentes were subject to foreign ridicule and attack, vehement denunciations by evangelical Protestant missionaries and established Catholics. In defense, Chapter 6 of the 1915 Session Laws of the State of New Mexico was passed, a bill defining as criminal libel the publication of intentionally malicious material concerning any fraternal or religious order or society.

Prior to the 1930s, moradas usually operated autonomously, having unofficial, friendly relations with other nearby groups; in 1931 a county organization, *La Fraternidad de Nuestro Padre Jesus del Condado de Taos*, was incorporated, with a council of local *Hermanos Mayores* and other elected representatives, governed by an elected *Hermano Mayor*

Principal. Other such organizations were established elsewhere. Both World Wars and the Depression deeply affected life in rural areas, and membership became more confined to the poorer classes.

In 1947 the Penitentes were officially recognized by the church in a statement by Archbishop Edwin V. Byrne, who declared that (1) the Penitentes were not a fanatical sect; (2) that they were related to the Third Order of St. Francis and organized to attain salvation through penance; (3) that penances were to be modified and private; and (4) that the Church had absolute authority over the Brotherhood. Don Miguel Archibeque, a longtime Santa Fe resident initiated into the *Hermandad* during Holy Week of 1910, who had devoted much of his life to modifying and organizing the Brotherhood in order to bring it back under Church direction, was appointed *Hermano Supremo*. Eight years passed before the last moradas joined the newly sanctioned Brotherhood. A systematic network of chapters became an official part of organized religion. Santa Fe remains the site for the annual general meeting and election, at which all *Hermanos Mayores* and council members are formally addressed by the Archbishop and other Church officials. Recently during the years of Archbishop Sanchez and Archbishop Sheehan, the Penitentes have been re-organized and further rules and regulations approved.

Penitente membership in 1960 was estimated at about two or three thousand Brothers associated with some 135 moradas. In her 1976 autobiography Georgia O'Keeffe wrote, "... one evening when I was living in Taos we walked back of the morada toward a cross in the hills. I was told that it was a Penitente cross ... large enough to crucify a man, with two small crosses — one on either side. It was in the late night and the cross stood out dark against the evening sky." In Abiquiu where she settled, there was the ruin of a morada, and, O'Keefe noted, "I saw the crosses so often — and often in unexpected places — like a thin dark veil of the Catholic church spread over the New Mexico landscape." She made several paintings of Penitente crosses with the mountains as the background. Interested in the culture of the place where she lived, she also painted kachina dolls; her fame brought attention to the area.

Haunted Mansions at the Perimeter

The Luna Mansion, Los Lunas

Domingo de Luna came to New Mexico on a land grant from the King of Spain in 1692, and a few years later Don Pedro Otero came to Valencia County under similar circumstances. Both families prospered and went into politics; the heads became friends and business associates. When Solomon Luna married Adelaide Otero in the late 1800s, what was known as the Luna Otero dynasty was founded.

The Santa Fe Railroad wanted right of way through the Luna property, and in exchange agreed to build a new family mansion to the specifications of Don Antonio Jose Luna. Don Antonio Jose died in 1881; his oldest son, Tranquilino, occupied the mansion until his death in Washington while serving in the legislature. Solomon then became head of the family, passing control to his nephew, Eduardo Otero, in the early 1900s.

During the 1920s the solarium was built, the front portico was added, and ironwork surrounded the property in antebellum Southern colonial style. Eduardo's wife Josefita, daughter of William R. Manderfield, founder of the *Santa Fe New Mexican*, was responsible for the improvements; she nurtured magnificent gardens, and was an artist who painted the murals and paintings still throughout the house in its current reincarnation as a restaurant.

And she has not left – though she had a fatal heart attack at the top of the stairs leading to the second floor bar room. She appears in the upstairs bar room, which was the master bedroom; employees and patrons have experienced cold chills, breathlessness, and sensed her presence. Dressed in white, her hair in a bun, she runs her fingers along the fringe of a lampshade as she strolls through the rooms, or sits by the window gazing onto the front lawn, where people can feel her gaze.

Light fixtures often have unscrewed bulbs – especially in the chandeliers. If the 300-year-old Manderfield table that seats fifteen is brought out of storage for private parties, eerie occurrences including shattered glass, the double doors leading to the kitchen opening by themselves, and water faucets turning on take place.

Territorial House

This ancient hacienda in Corrales was built in 1801 by Diego Montoya, and the Montoya family owned it until it was purchased in 1883 by Luis and Louisa Emberto. This couple's marriage had turned sour; both had lovers and fought bitterly, disturbing their son, who one night killed a woman he believed was his father's mistress at a social gathering. Luis moved out in a rage, believing his wife had put the son up to it, threatening to kill her and her lover.

On April 30, 1898, Luis did go to the house just after dark and shot her; their son fired at him several times but missed. An armed posse gunned him down the next day. Both Luis and Louisa could not be buried on consecrated ground, and were instead interred in unmarked graves on their property. Their ghosts frequently visit the banquet room of the current restaurant Rancho de Corrales operated there – the glowing red tip of a cigar floats about the room and chairs are stacked upon each other by an unseen presence.

The tree that stands in front of the hacienda was once used for hangings, and several other murder have been committed in the bar, so there are other ghosts. One of the ghosts is an old man in a rocking chair, another a woman in a long white dress. A child has also been heard crying in the rooms, and men are overheard talking in the bar when there is no one there.

Old Town is the heart of Albuquerque's heritage, since the first Spanish families settled near the banks of the Rio Grande in 1706. A colonial farming village and military outpost, the village took the traditional Spanish pattern of central plaza surrounded by church, homes, and government buildings – some old homes are still standing, many renovated into businesses selling art, turquoise and sterling silver jewelry, and clothing. The art galleries, restaurants, and retail shops of today were once wild saloons, rough gambling halls, and numerous 'houses of negotiated affection'. Meanwhile, the woman of the house ruled the grand mansions of a time, and many *still* have not relinquished their domain.

"Vengeful lovers, murdered soldiers, and mysterious specters await those who are brave enough to explore the secrets that lie within Old Town's darkest corners." *Old Town Ghost Tours*

The architecture of New Mexico changed after the raising of the American flag in 1846, as Anglo settlers arrived bringing new materials and architectural ideas based on the new world communities from which they came. The original destination of the railroad when it came in 1881 was the settlement along the Rio Grande River, but the soil was too soft and unstable for heavy locomotives, and track was laid on higher, more stable land to the east. The rail yard and depot became 'New Town' (now Downtown), and La Villa de Alburquerque became 'Old Town' and has remained Old Town since then.

The advent of the railroad caused imported supplies to replace local building materials. Many of the oldest buildings were constructed of adobe bricks and stucco; newer buildings dating from the late 1800s had wooden clapboard siding on the front and looked like other western towns of the time. As new designs supplanted native architecture, newer towns began to resemble the Midwest and the East. Millwork and brick and lime plasters were imported from St. Louis and Kansas City; adobe walls began to be capped with protective cornices of brick in ornamental patterns, and walls were coated with lime stucco. The Spanish small, grilled, glassless windows were replaced by double-hung, glazed sashes, often with slatted shutters on the outsides. Slender, squared columns replaced heavy hewn ones. Doors and windows were decorated with white-painted wood trim of Eastern precedent, though Hispanic Catholics still preferred blue oil paint, a color associated with the Virgin with a supposed power to ward off witches. In 1983, local paint manufacturers still offered blue tints labeled Taos, Laguna or Madonna.

Early visitors coming by train expected the buildings here to look different, so in the first decade of the twentieth century a reaction to architectural imports set in, with residents realizing that New Mexico's ancient forms not only had aesthetic value but were best adapted to the climactic conditions. Most structures in Old Town underwent the Pueblo Revival movement, being remodeled to add portals, vigas, and stucco. Victorian buildings still exist, for example behind or inside La Hacienda Restaurant (the peaked roof was removed); the Covered Wagon (white house complete with turret behind the facade); and La Placita Restaurant. Romero House has been remodeled into shops on the inside.

By the late nineteenth century, pueblos no longer needed to limit access to interiors for defense reasons, and adobe walls were opened up as additional doors and windows in pueblo buildings. Most early multiple dwellings were oriented to the sun, showing an early knowledge of passive solar heating fundamentals. Adobe is still used due to its economy, heat retention, insulation from noise, flexibility, and appropriateness to a Southwestern setting. Exterior adobe plaster does need to be replastered annually; it is estimated that weeds, wind, and water can return an abandoned adobe building to earth within twenty years.

The Savador Armijo House, 618 Rio Grande NW, is a twelve-room hacienda constructed of adobe enclosing a central patio, in the classic *placita* (little plaza) style, developed for defense against raiding by nomadic Native Americans. Facing toward old Town Plaza and San Felipe de Neri church, it was built in the changing times of the mid-1800s, and exhibits examples of exceptional architectural millwork. Church dignitaries, government officials, merchants, farmers, and stockmen all visited here.

Salvador Armijo was the grandson four times removed from the widow of Jose de Armijo, who arrived with four sons in New Mexico in 1695; one of the sons, Vicente Armijo, with his seven sons, became prominent in politics and business in Rio Abajo, the 'down river' area of New Mexico. Salvador was born into this family in 1794, joining his father and brothers in the family business of taking wagon trains of goods to and from Missouri and down into Mexico. In 1847 he married Paula Montoya and built the house in the fortress style of Spanish Colonial times, with adobe walls thirty-two inches thick. During the turmoil of the early settlement of Albuquerque, the building served as a fort and a refuge. Since glass for windows was not readily available, the house was very dark. One hundred acres around it were brought into cultivation.

Though business went well, he and Paula separated in 1848 after only one year of marriage. He then fell passionately in love with and married Dona Maria de las Nieves Sarracino – her name meaning Saracen of the Snows – member of another prominent family from Los Padillas south of Albuquerque. The house now was used as a trading post. During the volatile 1860s, though New Mexico did not side with the Confederacy, Salvador, his brother, and one other merchant suffered heavy losses when Union soldiers destroyed supplies in Albuquerque that the invading Confederate troops might need.

The ghost of a Confederate soldier was reported to have been seen on San Felipe Street within the boundaries of Old Town proper, sometimes on horseback, sometimes not. The ghost was believed to be one of the eight Rebels buried under the gazebo in the plaza, guarding two cannons that were buried in Old Town during Sibley's campaign in the Civil War (under certain circumstances, artillery units would rather bury their cannons before a hasty retreat than have them captured by the enemy and used against them later).

Sibley's campaign, the Confederate Texan invasion of New Mexico Territory in 1861-62, was the westernmost campaign of the Civil War. Sibley, who reached Albuquerque on March 2, 1862, to find the military post destroyed, remained there while his troops went on to capture a small post at Cubero, west of town, and confiscating and purchasing supplies locally. An advance party rode to and occupied the Santa Fe and its abandoned Fort Marcy, then attacking Fort Union, one hundred miles northeast.

On April 8, 1862, Colonel Canby, marching north with 1,200 Union troops, reached the city and sent a small artillery force against the Confederates in the Battle of Albuquerque. This drew the Confederates out of Santa Fe, then out of Albuquerque, by April 12, 1862.

One sighting was by a city street sweeper who claimed he was driving north on San Felipe when a man on horseback suddenly appeared in the road in front of him; he honked the horn but the rider and horse refused to move. He drove up on the curb to go around them. Disgruntled, he looked back after passing the rider, stopped the street cleaner and climbed out of the cab – to discover that horse and rider had disappeared. This, however, may be explained by police records from the time that show an arrest of a intoxicated man riding a horse on Central and Rio Grande Blvd. at 2:30 am, fifteen minutes after the sighting by the city employee.

Also, a city police officer responding to a call in Old Town saw a black shadow cross San Felipe Street in front of him. As the patrol car went through the 'cloud', the officer felt he had run over something; he stopped the car and got out to look. But nothing was there.

In 2003 a Confederate re-enactor and his wife had just finished having dinner at the Melting Pot and were walking back through Old Town to where they had parked their car; as they walked south on San Felipe street, he noticed a man in a Confederate uniform carrying an 1842 69 caliber musket, walking with a brisk stride, heading north. Curious about where the man had obtained the musket, the re-enactor crossed the street and called out to him. When the soldier didn't stop, the witness started to run after him; according to the re-enactor, the 'Confederate Soldier' turned a corner and vanished.

A tourist visiting Old Town in 2004 emailed the Southwest Ghost Hunters Association that he had heard the sounds of a horse following him while walking back to his car, but was unable to actually see it. He noted that the sound seemed to change, as if the horse was coming at him from different directions. In 2005 the source of the sound was replicated; after a rainstorm, water dripping into a gutter on Church Street creates the sound of a horse's hoofs. The sound's directional change is caused by the echo and the listener's position in Old Town; rain dripping down the gutter can be heard as far away as a block from the plaza when traffic noise from Rio Grande Boulevard is minimal.

Back to the Armijo family saga – in 1862 Salvador's daughter Piedad married Santiago Baca, who became involved in the family shipping business, now called Armijo y Hijo; branch stores were opened. Don Salvador left much of the business to his son, buying more land and a property on the plaza for warehouses and a store. His vineyards prospered, and by 1870 he was the biggest farmer in the Albuquerque area.

Soon after Piedad's marriage, Don Salvador and Dona Nieves separated – it took ten years to divide the property. The house and part of the farmlands were sold to her for $10,000, a huge sum at the time. In 1874 Piedad, Santiago, and their three children moved in with Dona Nieves, and in 1875 they began extensive remodeling. The house was done over in Territorial style, an adaptation of Greek Revival.

Piedad and Santiago became wealthy, involved in political activity, and dealt in real estate while operating the farm, winery, sheep ranch, and store. But in the mid-1890s, Santiago was embroiled in political battles and had family problems, resulting in a decline of his fortune.

Family squabbles caused the estate to come to ruin. Family members moving out, until in 1899 Meliton Chavez, married to Dona Nieves' granddaughter Francisca, bought the house when it was auctioned off on the steps of the Old Albuquerque Post Office for $1,125 in back taxes and debts. The couple moved in and in 1908, completed a major renovation, restoring the ruin to its present condition and remodeling it in conformity with its old character. The house again became a social center of the community. It remained in the family until 1977.

It is also the only building in Albuquerque with an intact *placita* (indoor patio). For the then Maria Teresa Restaurant, Roswell artist

John Miegs incorporated family heirlooms with period antique pieces, keeping the integrity of the house intact. The restaurant's main dining room was built around the tree within, sealing the *placita* and the newly formed room from the elements. In 1984 Old Town Development Company acquired the property and continued to preserve it.

The antique piano, which belonged to the original owners, has been heard playing in the early hours, when the diners and most of the staff had gone, and only a few people remained in the restaurant. A party has also been heard in the north boardroom, a spectral party with a guest list exclusive to the dead. When the floor boards in the bar were taken up for plumbing work, a disturbing cache of bones of various sizes was discovered – they turned out to be those of a large animal, perhaps a horse, mixed with human bones. Some say a spectral cowboy haunts the bar.

In the dining room hung a portrait of a woman in the Armijo family, labeled "Dona Jususita Salazar de Baca;" the eyes were piercing and the old woman genuinely beautiful. Apparently one of the waiters made fun of her looks, though, and from that point on he constantly tripped every time he walked in front of the portrait, dropping trays and falling to the floor. Finally, the ill-fated waiter walked out one night in the middle of his shift.

The Chacon room held the ghost of an elderly man in a dark suit, reflected in the mirrors – only the upper back and head could be seen. Sometimes after staff had arranged the table settings in this room, they'd move on to a task in another room and return to find the flatware piled haphazardly on the table. In a dining room adjacent to the Chacon room, a couple in 1993 and their waiter sighted the ghost of a middle aged Hispanic woman with light colored eyes and dark hair, wearing a red dress – she vanished, leaving behind a scent of flowery perfume.

The ghost of a woman wearing a white dress appeared in the Armijo room, which contains the majority of the original furnishings that belonged to the house. She took dinner and dessert orders for guests occasionally and also frequented another dining room named the Wine Press. She was accompanied by a gust of chilling air. She may be the ghost of Victoria, a servant girl who died of tuberculosis around 1783.

In the Zamora room, the ghost of a woman once appeared in the mirror, seated between two people of a party of six – but not in a chair, just sitting in space. She remained for about an hour and a half, until dessert, seeming to inspect the dinner plates and nod her approval, as if concerned about how patrons were being served. Obviously a woman of refinement, about thirty years old, she had long black hair and wore a sheer white dress. Among staff there was a saying, "The house accepts you when the ghost appears to you." With the restaurant now closed, one is left to wonder what these lively ghosts are doing for entertainment these days.

Albuquerque's Haunted Theatres

The Pueblo Deco that embellishes the **KiMo Theatre** was a short-lived style in America, fusing the spirit of Indian cultures with the exuberant Roaring Twenties style. The KiMo was built by Oreste Bachechi, who came to Albuquerque in 1885, one of the founding members of the Italian-American community. He had run a bar near the railroad tracks, been a liquor dealer and owned a grocery store, while his wife ran a dry goods store, before circa 1919 he operated the Bachechi Amusement Association, running the Pastime Theatre with Joe Barnett. By 1925, he decided to build the theatre of his dreams.

Carl Boller of the Boller Brothers firm was commissioned to design it, and traveled throughout New Mexico visiting the pueblos of Acoma, Isleta, Cibola, and the Navajo Nation for ideas. Panoramic murals in the interior painted by Prussian Carl von Hassler depicted the Seven Cities of Cibola, fabled for their richness in the first written accounts of New Mexico when a Spanish ship sank off the coast of Florida and four survivors made their way across the continent to the Gulf of California, reaching Mexico City after nine years. The legend drew Coronado here to search for them. Chandeliers were shaped like war drums and death canoes; wrought-iron railings depicted birds, and rows of garlanded steer skulls held eerie, glowing eyes. Every design, medallion, and terra cotta relief had historical significance. Colors were chosen as part of the Indian vocabulary. The theatre was a labor of love completed in less than a year, with opening night in fall of 1927. The name is a combination of to words literally meaning 'mountain lion', but more liberally interpreted as 'King of its Kind'.

On the balcony of the Kimo Theatre

On Thursday afternoon, Aug. 2, 1951, a six-year-old boy named Bobby Darnall was watching a show in the balcony section when he became frightened by something on the screen; he ran downstairs to the lobby, just as a water heater exploded behind the wall. Eight people were injured, some very seriously, and Bobby died.

The 'Bobby Shrine' started when morning crews discovered that the leftover doughnuts they had abandoned had been bitten into or had disappeared the next day. Doughnuts began to be tied to an exposed water pipe backstage, and the stage crew began leaving one uneaten doughnut in remembrance for the dead boy's spirit. The collection grew; sweets and toys were added. In 1974, a crewmember removed the desiccated objects in disgust – and immediately, accidents began to happen. Props that had been well anchored fell over; electrical cables sparked and blew up; actors tripped and fell over invisible objects. Some saying they felt invisible hands push them. Theatre staff restored the little shrine, and shows seemed to go much more smoothly – actors did not forget lines, and lighting and sound functioned properly. There are even lipstick kisses on the wall, left by ballerinas who performed at the KiMo.

There have been numerous sightings of the ghost of the little boy, playing and scampering on the stairs, wearing a striped shirt and jeans. The most recent sighting was in 2003. There are two other entities that seem to be much older than the young boy who make appearances – one is a woman dressed as an early settler would be.

The Wool Warehouse Theater at 201 Marquette NW was constructed in 1928-29, featuring Egyptian motifs and Roaring Twenties art deco, creating a facility inviting for weddings and parties. It was used as an office for the Bond family wool dealers until 1974, also housing offices of the NM Cooperative Wool Marketing Association. It has served as a dinner theatre and restaurant, and is a National Historic Landmark building currently owned by the Doubletree Hotel.

The wool industry in New Mexico grew between the two world wars, and Albuquerque became the center of processing and distribution in New Mexico, aided by the proximity of the railroad. But after 1942 production began to fall, unable to keep up with demand – growers blamed limited access to grazing lands as part of the problem. Synthetic fabrics spelled the end of wool marketing.

When the building was in use as a dinner theatre in 1984, an unidentified ghost of a heavyset male in a cream, double-breasted suit appeared near the theater stage during performances, sometimes interacting with performers and patrons. He may be the ghost of an employee who committed suicide after his wife divorced him and he lost his job. Actors have felt presences and been touched by unseen hands. A ghost shouted at one actor. A ghostly woman was heard screaming in the restroom on occasion and the door would inexplicably jam at other times, trapping living women inside. Cold spots seem to move about the building, most often being just to the right of the stage.

The caretaker of the **Albuquerque Little Theatre** from the 1950s until his death, Manuel Jaramillo, had his ashes spread beneath the trap door below the stage. An apricot tree he planted still stands by the theatre. His family organizes an annual Christmas memorial for him at the theatre, and ALT members who knew him say they can feel his presence in the theatre, where doors close and open of their own accord. He is a benevolent spirit, still keeping his eye on the place.

Directors and actors at **Highland High School Theatre** leave a 'ghost light' on the center of their stage to prevent the crew from walking into a dark and ghost-ridden theatre in the morning. It is believed that the ghost of a drama student who committed suicide still roams the stage.

At **Del Norte High School Theatre**, actors leave a penny on the first step of the stairs leading to the light and sound booth and never step on it; this is to appease the techie ghost, said to lurk above the stage on the catwalk. This ghost has the ability to grant a successful run or to condemn a play.

Manzano High School Theatre has a ghost named Allen, on whose behalf the cast and crew keep a flag at half-mast backstage, raising it to full height before a performance. If this were not done, Allen would cause fuses to burst and furniture to creak.

The Albuquerque Press Club, 201 Highland Park SE, was built as a family residence by architect Charles Whittlesey in 1903 – a three story frame structure designed after a Norwegian villa. In 1908 the Whittleseys sold it to Theodore S. Woolsey Jr., who owned it for the next twelve years.

Albuquerque was known for its good climate, conducive to the treatment of diseases. Two sanitariums were located near the house, and it was later leased by Woolsey to those who came to convalesce. A nurse named Clifford who had come West with a patient told her suitor, Arthur B. Hall, that if he bought the house she would marry him; Hall did so in 1920, and Clifford lived in the house for the next forty years, remodeling it and bringing about interior style changes with predominantly Native American motifs. Early New Mexican artists often worked and painted on the wide porch, and the Halls also collected Chinese and Indian furniture.

Clifford was divorced from Hall in 1930, and remarried to Herbert McCallum in 1935, but this too ended in divorce in 1938. For income, she rented out portions of the house, framing off the south porch and sealing off part of the first level to form a separate apartment. The stable as well was remodeled into an apartment complex. By the mid-forties, Clifford was working for Vanlandingham Studios, first as a seamstress and then as the owner. Redecoration of her home continued, with marble topped European pieces filling the main room. The house was a showplace that Clifford opened to many people, including international guests. The Mayo brothers visited, as did politicians.

Clifford sold the house in 1960 to Zeta Mu Zeta House Corporation of Lambda Chi Alpha Fraternity; in 1973 it was purchased by the Albuquerque Press Club.

Clifford's ghost, known as 'Emma' or 'Mrs. M.' from her third marriage to McCallum, still wanders about in a black dress, her high-heeled shoes audible on the wood floor, overseeing her domain. Shot glasses of gin are left for her on the bar. Sometimes she drinks them, sometimes not. She has also been known to play a few notes on the old piano in the main room of the house.

The front room of the building that houses **Alfredo's Restaurant** on Charlevoix Street, once nicknamed Burro Alley due to laws that prohibited them in the plaza, was constructed prior to 1706 as a Native American residence. Made of adobe bricks mortared with mud, then protected with a layer of mud or cement, much of the original walls remain, and the original *vigas* are still visible in the ceiling. Kiva style fireplaces were the prime source of heat. When the building was turned into a Spanish fort just before the settlement of Albuquerque was founded, the back of the building was where the horse corral was located. After the fort was abandoned, the building became a stagecoach stop. The horse corral has been built over and is now the main room of the building where bands play in its current incarnation as a restaurant; it has previously been inhabited by various mercantile shops and a bicycle shop.

There is a ghost that haunts this café, perhaps a long passed away Native American who still moves about the grounds – but the most popular theory is that it is a Spanish soldier who once occupied the fort. The door to the power box inexplicably flies open with great force on occasion. Often when this occurs, the heating is turned on. Lights turn on and off, apparently by themselves, throughout the entire location. Disembodied voices that sound like they are speaking Spanish, but are mumbled enough so that exactly what is being said is hard to understand, have been heard coming from the kitchen area. On occasion the sound of the voices is preceded by the uneasy feeling that one is being watched. Sudden cold 'breezes' have also been experienced twice near the counter.

The coffee house is only one small part of the ancient Spanish fort, which extended down toward the east to San Felipe Street and turned south. Other shops within this area have also reported unusual occurrences similar in nature to those that occur here. Locations on San Felipe Street seem to be more consistently active, perhaps due to the location of living quarters and defensive positions when the area was a Spanish fort.

To the Present Day: Chapel of our Lady of Guadalupe

La Capilla de Nuestra Senora de Guadalupe, the tiny Chapel of our Lady of Guadalupe erected in 1975 and tucked away at 404 San Felipe NW in the Patio Escondido in Old Town, was designed and built by Sister Giotto as part of a larger project, an art school which she had established in 1969. Sister Giotto, born in 1927 and raised in Chicago where she attended high school at Chicago's famous Art Institute, had a conversion experience when she was seventeen, after listening to the boys coming home from WWII and praying for them daily. She entered a Dominican convent and studied in Florence, Italy, eventually receiving her M.F.A. in Wisconsin. Returning to her alma mater in Florence, she held the position of Dean of the Art Department at Villa Schifanoia for eight years. In 1965, the Vatican urged that schools of sacred arts should be set up wherever possible, and Sister Giotto got permission to set up such a school. The Sagrada Arts School eventually consisted of studios, apartments, the chapel, and even a restaurant called Joseph's Table.

This structure is haunted by an apparition called the lady in black, often seen seated on the far right bench of the chapel, weeping. The ghost wears a long black dress and her face is concealed by a dark veil. Often she is mistaken for a real person, and sometimes ignored, until she mysteriously vanishes. The apparition is not menacing or threatening. Those who encounter her have said that there is a deep sense of sadness that emulates from her.

One popular notion is that the ghost is crying for the victims of TWA flight 260 that crashed into the Sandia Mountains on February 19, 1955, killing all thirteen passengers and three crew members on board. Wreckage of the plane can be seen from the Sandia Peak Tramway, which is the world's longest passenger aerial tramway and also has the world's third longest single span, stretching from the northeast edge of the city to the crestline of the Sandia Mountains. In this variant, the ghost is seen to enter the alleys that lead to the *capilla* only on the anniversary of the crash. Another theory is that the ghost only appears in times of tragedy – a fatal crash on the interstate or some other catastrophe, when her apparition appears to mourn the loss.

La Capilla de Nuestra Senora de Guadalupe, 404 San Felipe NW.

The First Highways

El Camino Real

Don Juan de Oñate first 'blazed' the northern portion of the **El Camino Real**, the route created using a series of Native American footpaths used for trade between the indigenous people of Tenochititlán/Mexico City and Chaco. Don Juan de Oñate claimed the land for Spain. He had traveled on orders from King Philip to discover a route to Nuevo España (New Spain – what is now New Mexico). Earlier explorers, like Coronado, had only glimpsed the terrain. His caravan consisted of about 175 soldiers and their families (exact numbers are unknown as many hid until the King's auditors left, since they were considered criminals; many were convicts from Central Mexico who had chosen military service over jail in the capital) and over 5,000 head of cattle and sheep. Linking Mexico with the United States, the trail extended from Mexico City and the port city of Veracruz to El Paso, Texas, and San Juan Pueblo, New Mexico, a distance of over 1,500 miles. Until about 1885 colonists from Mexico and Spain entered New Mexico along El Camino Real; many of the people living in the Southwest today are decendents of these early settlers. In less than four hundred years, ruts from the hooves of mules and horses and simple wooden wheels were extended into the railroad and interstate highways of the present day. Interstate 25, from Las Cruces to Santa Fe, closely parallels the route of El Camino Real through New Mexico. The name El Camino Real de Tierra Adentro is Spanish for 'The Royal Road of the Interior' and it is now a legislated national historic trail, the country's oldest and longest continuously used 'highway', bringing Europeans to New Mexico twenty-two years before the Mayflower arrived on the East Coast. Various haunted locations dot this ancient roadway, a number of which are discussed throughout this book.

Route 66

Route 66, or transcontinental highway US 66, came relatively late, mapped out as a road from Chicago to Los Angeles in the 1930s. It followed the Chicago, Rock Island, and Pacific Railroad to Santa Rosa, but for the 160 miles between Santa Rosa and Laguna, paralleled no railroad right of way. West of Laguna and on to Los Angeles, it followed the Santa Fe Railroad tracks. Famous as a route to California during the Dust Bowl and Depression days, by the 1960s it had become the major highway of the mountain Southwest. This resulted in a need for hotels, many of which were converted mansions.

Haunted Hotels

A forty-room adobe house was originally constructed on the site of the **Böttger Mansion**, which until 1845 served as the residence of the territorial governor while in New Mexico, when it was a territory of Mexico. Charles Böttger, a wool exporter from Germany who had made his fortune after migrating to New Jersey, moved to the Rio Grande Valley in the 1890s to be closer to the Native American sheep ranchers and the wool supply. He worked for Tom Post, who owned the Sunnyside Tavern across the street on land that is now the Plaza Vieja parking lot. After the death of Tom Post, Böttger married Mr. Post's widow, Michaela, and acquired the property, which then extended from approximately South Plaza Street south to Central Avenue and San Pasquale Street west to Romero Street. In approximately 1908 the adobe house was demolished to make room for the new Böttger Mansion. Of the four original mansions in Old Town, only this one at 110 San Felipe NW remains virtually in the same condition as when built. It was occupied for three generations by the Böttgers.

Böttger wanted his new home, designed by local architect Edward Cristy in the American Foursquare style popular when New Mexico was still a U.S. territory, to contain the most modern conveniences.

Bottger Mansion, 110 San Felipe NW.

It was the first residence in Albuquerque to have gas lighting; the original gas pipes are still hidden inside ceilings. Speaking tubes ran to all the rooms, the three main rooms featured pressed-tin ceilings, and a dumb waiter carried meals to the upper floor. The mansion was one of very few homes in Albuquerque to have a basement, with both a coal-fired central heater and a coal cellar located there; the only fireplace in the entire mansion was located in the parlor.

In the mid-1930s, a Böttger grandson painted a mural of New Mexico mountains around the upper wall of the Linda Lee room. Charles Böttger was the first to purchase an automobile in Albuquerque, and convinced other property owners to donate land for the creation of San Felipe Street.

The Böttger Mansion became a hotel in the 1940s, which Machine Gun Kelly checked into in the late forties, and in the late fifties a prominent Italian family rented it for a large wedding at which Frank Sinatra performed. When Elvis Presley did two shows in Albuquerque in 1955, he stayed at the Bottger. Janis Joplin stayed here in the 1960s. In approximately 1970, due to a family dispute relating to inheritance, the Böttger Mansion remained vacant for several years and was sold outside the family. Over the years the open front portal was closed in and the house became home to a small colony of Buddhists, an art gallery, restaurant, beauty parlor, and several other business ventures. It became a bed and breakfast around 1989. It had escaped the Pueblo Revival renovation and preserves its Victorian atmosphere. Located on Historic Route 66, the Böttger Mansion is on the National Register of Historic Places and is the only accommodation in the Old Town Historic District.

There are believed to be six different ghosts at the mansion: Charles and Michaela Böttger; their daughter Dorothy, who is said to have died of pneumonia after being locked out; a native woman who fell down the stairs to her death; a 'grandmother ghost' heard sighing, perhaps in lamentation that her children intended to sell the property after her death; and the 'lover ghost', who is reputed to lie down next to young women while they sleep, and then disappear when the lights come on.

La Posada de Albuquerque, built in 1939 by New Mexico native Conrad Hilton as the Albuquerque Hilton Hotel, was the fourth Hilton built and the first built outside of Texas. On the corner of Second and Copper in downtown Albuquerque, it was convenient to Route 66 and the Atchison, Topeka, and Santa Fe Railroad depot. Its two-story lobby, arches, hand carved beams, and balconies overlooking the lobby made it one of Albuquerque's finer places to stay, the first building in Albuquerque and New Mexico with air conditioning and the tallest in both the city and state upon opening on June 9, 1939.

After almost thirty years, Hilton needed a larger facility in Albuquerque and the downtown property was sold, renamed the Hotel Plaza. Railroad and bus companies leased several floors for their crews and drivers in the early eighties, and the hotel was developing a less than desirable reputation when it finally closed its doors. With a grant from the City of Albuquerque and assistance from the National Register of Historic Places, a full-scale restoration began, with the goal of returning the hotel to the glory of its early days.

An apparition of a woman in a 1940s style hat and dress has appeared on the seventh floor, as well as an apparition of a elderly woman wearing a pink dress. The majority of ghostly encounters occur on the 4th and 7th floors, although there have been some reports of activity in the 2nd floor ballroom. Manifestations occur in the late evening or afternoon.

Desert Sands Motel, located at 5000 Central Ave SE, is a cheap and easy place to stay when headed west on I40. Visitors who got the corner room of the center building on the first floor experienced cold spots, heard voices in the bathroom, the water ran by itself, the TV kept turning on and off on its own, changing channels by itself, and the door kept unlocking. One guest in Room 109 felt someone ... some*thing* watching her, the TV set stayed on after she unplugged it, and something yanked her hair while she was in the shower.

Radisson Hotel – On the first floor of the hotel one can hear scratching noises and slamming doors above one late at night, even if there is no one renting the room above. There is loud yelling and screaming in rooms that are vacant, and sometimes women are shaken until they wake up by what feels like children's hands. The third floor (which no one is supposed to be on) is the only floor that has not been remodeled. When elevator doors open there, one is hit with a gust of hot air. Walking further through the floor, there are the remains or what used to be a bar. The bar's counter top is in perfect condition, but the rest is completely destroyed. In the corner of the bar is what appears to be newly broken glass. No one knows how it got there, because no employees have been up there recently, and none of the windows have been broken.

Ramada Hotel – According to one of the staff, the corner room of this big hotel is haunted by a young, broken-hearted lady. In this ill-fated room, the young woman's heartless lover killed her because he wanted out of her life. She is said to only be on the bottom floor, where she haunts the lobby and the room where she was killed. When service ladies went to clean the corner room, they would find it in turmoil. The bed sheets were thrown all over the place, the TV was knocked to the floor, and the curtains were torn up. This activity went on for so long that management finally closed off the room and doesn't rent it out anymore. But often, staff members still look in on the corner room. They continue to find it in complete disarray. One wonders whether the violent rearrangement of the room is caused by the broken-hearted woman or her heartless ex-lover.

Ghost-ridden Albuquerque Institutions

And then there are the ghosts that haunt Albuquerque institutions, past and present. The area of the **Bernalillo County Courthouse**, where the divorce court once was, is haunted by the apparition of a little girl. In 2003 the Community Service group was cleaning up, and collectively witnessed strange things. A little girl, perhaps six or seven years old, with blond hair in pigtails and wearing a school uniform, was reported standing in one of the dark halls. An aura of sadness radiated from her. When the witnesses smiled at her, she vanished.

A cold spot in another hall was experienced, with no vent or source to explain it. The workers were taking a break in one of the rooms when an old law book, circa 1920s, went skittering down the hall, coming to a stop in the cold zone. Two people reportedly died of heart attacks in the building – a Sheriff at his desk in the basement and another man on an upper floor. Employees have tried doing little 'tests' – placing objects in certain places and placing a dry eraser on a door knob, etc., and then returning to find these objects moved. The basement also reputedly has ghosts, and objects are moved about in locked rooms. Boxes that were taped closed are found opened and the contents strewn about.

Bernalillo County Courthouse

Carrie Tingley Children's Hospital, 1127 University NE, originally a children's polio hospital located in Truth or Consequences, moved to its current location in 1981. Staff and patients have reported 'glowing rooms' in unused portions of the hospital, as well as invisible 'force fields' 'that do not allow one to pass'; these fields also make a static/hissing sound when encountered. There are sounds of crying, the throb of heartbeats, and black robed figures are seen in darkened halls.

It is rumored that a patient at the abandoned **Insane Asylum** on the corner of Edith and Osuna killed several patients and staff in a particularly gruesome manner, and after this the asylum was forced to close down. Both a figurative and a literal dark cloud hangs over the place, which has appeared in pictures as well. The building is owned by neighbors who are actually the Banditos motorcycle gang; they are strict about trespassing, and don't mind releasing their Rottweilers on anyone who enters their property.

At the **Albuquerque Job Corp Center**, a convent in the 1800s that cared for small children, 'Sister M' went insane and killed her charges, tossing bodies into the well; these skeletons were discovered when residents installed a swimming pool where the well was located. A spectral woman has been seen by the lunchroom, a nun that is sometimes carrying a baby, and the cries of children are heard.

In the **Johnson Gym**, University of New Mexico, at night, after closing, one feels a strong presence and senses being followed and watched. Also, shadows appear in the corner of the eye, and immediately disappear if looked at directly. Urban legend has it that a murder took place many years ago, or that a student hung herself in one of the locker rooms.

San Pedro Library – There is a tale that at night one would hear a dead librarian saying "please come check out a book!" The lights turn on and off and things control themselves; her dead children slither around while darkening the room.

UNM Children's Psychiatric Hospital – Employees who work here know about the seclusion suite being haunted. Numerous employees have witnessed water turning on and off by itself, lights flickering on and off, doors lock and cannot be unlocked by humans, and small black footprints walking across the bathroom floor. In one instance, the security cameras were blocked out by a black image and a figure walking towards the camera lens, which appeared larger and larger when one looked at the monitor televisions. Numerous patients who have stayed in the seclusion suite claim they cannot sleep due to visual 'hallucinations' which may actually be ghosts.

Xilinx – This building is now a technology development center, but once served as a mental health hospital. Staff members hear mysterious banging sounds throughout the building (mostly in the bathroom), groans are heard in the courtyard, and whispers in the back office area. Objects have moved of their own accord, and shadowy figures are seen moving along the hallways.

Another Infusion: Culture and Politics

Belly dancing has thrived in the area since the 1960s, arriving with immigrants who brought Islamic tradtions with them to add to the mixture of spiritual beliefs.

"I want to archive everything artistic since our countries have been at war – music, dance, jewelry – an accurate history of achievements in this country, in the fields of literature and medicine," says Tasha Banat, who runs the Near East Art Alliance from her Albuquerque home. "The zero, alchemy, coffee – all are Arab inventions."

Tasha is named after the destroyed city of Dahaisha in Palestine from which her mother was evicted in 1943. Born in 1948, she was in a camp before Israel was created. Her parents brought her to New York in 1951, but every summer until her grandmother died in 1958, she would go to visit her in the camp just outside Bethlehem, for a long time thinking this was what 'summer camp' was.

"Music and dance was what we brought along, I had no toys," Tasha says. Later she was to become active with belly dance, known from hieroglyphic pictures to be as old as mankind, though images show dancers as exclusively female. In the camp community men participated in a combination of belly dance and folk dance – the music, like Arabic rock'n'roll. This way, Tasha says, culture was preserved; though the preconception of 'oriental' dance derived from the British/French invasion after the Ottoman Empire – cabaret, can-can, nightclub style entertainment – its popularity brought a heightened awareness of Middle Eastern textiles and music.

Tasha feels she became socially political upon moving to Florida in 1958; when asked, "where are you from?" at her answer, "B'ldesham," no one could place her. Olive-skinned, she would go to the drinking fountain marked 'colored' because there was no line, but would be shouted at for this – she wanted to go back to Palestine, where one knew one's friends and enemies! She thought America violent and vulgar; with desegregation, she became socially active. Wage slavery seen in the North bothered her. When she was a little older, the Cubans started coming – and hijackings and kidnapping became popular. She spent much time trying to understand the situation. "Middle East," she explains, was a term coined by a reporter in 1922 to describe the area of Lebanon, Jordan, Palestine/Israel, Syria, and part of Iraq. Expanding and contracting borders depended on how it was seen – before, there was only a Near East and a Far East.

Graduating the youngest ever at sixteen, Tasha won a scholarship to the Pasadena Playhouse acting school in 1965 – like all teenagers, she wanted to get away from her parents, and moved to California with alacrity. As a college student, she heard Arabic music coming from a restaurant, and entered. The men asked, can you do *raks b'ton?* and she said, what's that? Tasha discovered conscious and subliminal Arabic roots; having been taught the songs by her grandmother, and knowing *depke*, regional dance, she mixed this and cabaret style as a money-maker, her first costume made by a kitchen worker. The audience was 100% Arabic. While studying singing and acting, she made money belly dancing.

Later she developed her own style, Lebanese in origin. She studied muscles, bones, and the body, finding belly dance therapeutic. She lives and teaches in Albuquerque, and has a troupe that is Arabic. Performing in Iraq and the Middle East, she "had to buy a lot of gold and wear it out!"

Tasha feels a need for definition – the Middle East doesn't really have belly dance. She thinks the music, history, and meaning of each dance should be documented. Politically active in the Arab community, she also teaches Arab children, but found a stigma to overcome: parents wanted their children to know the traditional dance, but midriff-exposing belly dance costumes were not acceptable. "It's two communities that do not meet," she says.

With the second Iraqi war in 2003, UNM students were being picked up and treated unfairly. Tasha, as a member of the American Arab Anti-Discrimination Committee, filed a complaint against the Albuquerque Police Department for profiling Arabs. With this case, the Independent Review Officer was able to establish a Racial Profiling Task Force in New Mexico, providing classes to police on different philosophies and how to deal with Muslims. The task force receives complaints, researches, and funds are awarded to communities for regular courses.

"The best way to combat bigotry is through knowledge and compassion," Tasha says, having established the Near East Arts Alliance in 2001 to promote cultural, political, and religious sources. Through the archive, books, articles, and videos are available to scholars nationally, materials are provided so that Islam can be taught from a different angle. And Tasha continues to teach belly dance, Arab instruments, and drums.

For Women: The Alchemy of Transformation

Belly dance has thrived in the area since the sixties; with a surge in Albuquerque/Santa Fe/Taos in the last five years, belly dance is almost mainstream. Classes are held in high schools, the YMCA, the university, and private studios. Mary Ann Thomson has taught belly dance at UNM for thirty years. With her passion for music, she studied drumming and tambourine, teaching these and *zils*, the finger cymbals. "You used to not be able to get a job if you couldn't play *zils*," she laughs.

Flo Bargar and her husband opened Old World Imports in Albuquerque, selling goods from Afghanistan, India, and Pakistan, in 2000, because of their interest in travel and the arts. Belly dancers came in looking for accessories and jewelry. Flo was invited to a class – and became addicted and obsessed, she laughs. She teaches fusion/tribal style belly dance, purely an American invention stemming from East

Indian and classical Persian as well as Middle Eastern roots, using an improv language of movements, linked as a group process. Belly dance is very *accepting*, Flo feels; one can be any age, shape or size; little or no experience is required. It's for women themselves, their group, tribe, a support group to strengthen and empower themselves.

Flo uses earthy music, drums – mixing world fusion, lounge, chill, and Bollywood. " 'The funnest part is dressing up,' a student tells me – Old World Imports now makes custom costumes and provides sarongs, beaded and mirrored belts, embroidered dress fronts, all the paraphernalia for splendor."

Ghosts and Ghouls According to Islam

Muslim thought is that superstition and belief in ghosts were banished with Islam. In pre-Islamic folklore the Arabic word *djinn*, or genie in English, described a magical fiery spirit, or race of supernatural beings. *Djinn* also included anything which had the connotation of concealment, invisibility, seclusion, and remotenenss. Interestingly, the English word genie comes from the French *génie*, meaning a spirit of any kind, in turn coming from the Latin word *genius* which originally represented a tutelary or guardian spirit thought to be assigned to one at birth.

According to the Qur'an, *djinn* are creatures of free will, made from 'smokeless fire' by God (the literal translation being "subtle fire," or a fire which does not give itself away through smoke). Man (Adam) was created from sounding clay like the clay of pottery, and *djinns* from a smokeless flame of fire. Free choice was first invoked by Iblis when God commanded him to bow to Adam and he refused. Having refused to obey God's order, he was thrown out of Paradise and called Shaitan, or Satan. The Qur'an states that Muhammad was sent as a prophet to both 'humanity and the Djinn'.

Djinn live in communities or tribes that have boundaries, following religions, and having the same ranks in armies as humans do;

because they are mass-less and can fit into any space, they can settle into any location, from a vast territory to a tiny hole, as in a lamp. They are invisible to humans, but can see humans; they occasionally, accidentally or deliberately, come into view or contact with humans. They have a much longer life span than humans, some of those said to be still alive having seen Muhammad. Djinn can take on the form of humans and animals, but do not take on the forms of prophets and the 12 Imams of Shi'ite Islam. They can also be summoned by humans.

In the TV show 'I Dream of Jeannie', Jeannie, the genie, frequently was given a request, but the requestor never quite got what was asked for, as she was always creating unintentional mischief. Those who seek aid from a *djinn* will find deception and a twisted type of aid that doesn't really meet the original request. Humans attempting to perform black magic would call a dark *djinn*, specializing in such deeds as influencing a marriage to end in divorce. The *djinn* can also act as a supernatural thief.

Shaitan, the longest lived of all the *djinn*, antagonize humans. They are not kind beings who accidentally mess up on occasion. They live in mountains where even rocks and water are hot. Masters of deception, well known for their pride, they can manipulate the pride of man to turn him away from his fate. Often appearing as beautiful women but retaining some part of an animal form on their body, they have human worshipers and slaves, can disappear in a cloud of smoke, and travel on clouds of hot air. They may appear as a jackal, or are seen as riding black camels, and use disease as a weapon in many instances.

Ghouls, or Ghillan, the name meaning 'to seize', are another type of *djinn*, the most depraved. They stalk trackless wastes of the desert, preying upon the living and the dead. They may only eat what they have killed, or the meat of a dead creature that has not had the name of a protective deity spoken over it. Very intelligent, they behave like animals when a crazed lust for food is upon them. They superstitiously consider their hospitality inviolable, and if offered salt, will not attack the individual who offered it, or his household. Ghillan often appear as pilgrims who join caravans and fall upon their hosts if not treated with due hospitality. They attack individuals or small groups, may seek out grave sites to devour the newly dead or retrieve them for use by evil wizards or other diabolical masters. They can change into vultures, flocking with real ones to hover over battlefields and dying travelers; as beasts of burden, they always have asses' hooves. The only way to kill a ghoul is by striking it down with a single blow – striking twice will invest new life. As immigrants have brought Islamic spiritual beliefs filled with djinns and ghillans with them to Albuquerque, is it possible these creatures have traveled to New Mexico as well?

The Tibetan Migration

Both Santa Fe and Albuquerque were designated cluster sites for Tibetan refugees in 1992, and approximately forty Tibetans initially came to New Mexico as a result, enriching the already diverse cultural landscape. As they became American citizens, they brought their families and established firm roots for a Tibetan community.

From 1983 to 1996, six stupas (originally mound-like structures containing Buddhist relics, an ancient from of mandala, later embellished architecturally to become places of worship) were built in a line roughly following the Rio Grande river from Albuquerque north to Crestone, Colorado. As is traditional in Buddhist countries, hundreds of monks supported by devoted lay followers contributed to the construction. Each community of dharma students, or *sangha*, found ways of meeting the rigorous, precise, and expensive demands of stupa building. Lamas provided direction at each step, from fire *pujas* (prayer ceremonies) for fair weather to the construction of hundreds of thousands of *tsa-tsas* – tiny clay stupas – to be sealed in *bumpas*, spherical rooms below the spires. There is even a contested, nameless stupa that was enveloped by Petroglyph National Park after The National Park Service acquired the property of Harold Cohen and Arriam Emery, six months after the consecration of the ten-foot-high stupa that had taken them eleven years to build. Cohen and Emory lost their home and their battle to retain the stupa, spending money they had saved for a future Padmasambhava Center in litigation. Lama

Rinchen Thuntsok of Nepal, who had aided in building the stupa and had consecrated it in 1989, advised them to view the process as a lesson in impermanence.

Tibetan families in New Mexico continue the centuries-old tradition of making carpets; master artisans hand-card, spin, and dye the lanolin-rich local wool. Willem Reeders, called Liu-Siong after his great-uncle, came to Albuquerque in 1972 and opened the Garuda Studio of Tibetan Tai Chi in 1985. He was also a refugee from the Communist takeover of China in 1949. One of the few who completed his training at Shao-lin Temple in China, he says, "Even the Tibetans aren't doing Tibetan any more."

Thangka Paintings

RigDzin Dharma Foundation is a Tibetan Buddhist Dharma Center founded in Albuquerque in 2005 that offers teachings by visiting lamas from Tibet. Coming from hostile and harsh terrain, with the world's most formidable mountains, enormous deserts, and vast lakes swept by fierce winds, Tibetans have an instinctive respect for nature, with veneration only one step away. The Tibetan pantheon holds terrifying deities, depicted on *thangkas*, religious paintings that offer a beauty believed to be a manifestation of the divine, and thus are visually stimulating. They are three-dimensional composite items, consisting of a painted or embroidered (more recently printed) picture panel, a textile mounting on two wooden dowels with a silk cover, with metal or wooden decorative knobs on the bottom dowel.

Important articles of the tent culture of nomadic monastic groups in medieval Tibet, these perform several different functions; images of deities were used as teaching tools in depicting the life (or lives) of the Buddha, describing historical events concerning important Lamas, or retelling myths associated with other deities. On religious holidays of the lunar cycle, specific thangkas are removed from storage at the monastery, unrolled, hung up in shrine halls, and then taken down to be stored once more. The devotional images are the centerpiece during rituals or ceremonies and are seen as mediums through which pilgrims can offer prayers or make requests. When a Tibetan dies, the family may commission a thangka to remember him.

The painting is laid out on a systematic grid of angles and intersecting lines, with the skilled thangka artist working to iconographic specifications and choosing from a variety of predesigned items for the composition, ranging from alms bowls and animals, to the shape, size, and angle of a figure's eyes, nose, and lips. Tibetan thangka painters and the tailors who mount the work often have differing intents, skills, and training, as there are regional and doctrinal differences in style. The process requires a deep understanding of the symbolism and allusion in the work undertaken in order to capture the essence or spirit of it. Strict guidelines are laid out in Buddhist scripture. In Tibet, it was traditional for one son from each family to enter the monastery. The artist is generally a trained monk who has sufficient religious understanding, knowledge, and background to create an accurate and appropriate thangka for reflection and meditation. Thangka painting may also be a family tradition, passed down for generations.

Deities and Symbols

The peaceful and wrathful forms of Tibetan deities coexist, both being part of the same thing at the same time – but not in the same place, since their existence is relational. Deities are regarded not so much as gods but as "aspects of the divine" manifest in each part of the entire non-dual universe, which includes individual humans. The popular Green Tara, for instance, is thought to be incarnated in all good women, and has a moral base in historic persons such as the Nepali and Chinese princesses who married the king Song-tsen Gampo, credited with introducing Buddhism to Tibet.

Buddhism evolved from Hinduism, which may be seen as starting in about 2500 B.C. during the period of highly developed civilization in the valley of the Indus. Natural phenomena were seen as divine forces; traces of animal and snake worship, as well as of a Mother Goddess, remain. Prayers developed, with charms and magic designs which were probably the origin of mandalas; the oldest of which was the upright triangle, symbol of the Goddess of Fertility. The symbols used in ritual grew and evolved into Tantra. The Mother Goddess of nature, which provides everything for the sustenance of life, became the Absolute Power.

In about 2000 B.C., natural forces assumed a human form. From the oral tradition, the Vedas originated, holy texts with varying contents and different nature that were written down between approximately 1200 B.C. (the Rig-Vedas) and 400 B.C. (the Upanishads). Only after the Vedic Age did female deities become subordinate to male figures, and the inverted triangle came to represent the female principle. Agni (fire), Surya (the sun), and Indra became superior to the other gods, later being replaced. Destiny was seen as being in the hands of the gods, who must be appeased through sacrifice and ritual, and only priests could serve as intermediaries.

Gradually man acquired a more central position and the practice of sacrifice was supplemented or replaced by the practice of devotion, resulting in the epic books written from approximately 400 B.C. to 600 A.D.: the *Ramayana,* devoted to the seventh incarnation of Vishnu, Rama; the *Mahabharata,* following the development of the nation as it became well-armed and strategically strong and conquered the south, absorbing its gods into the pantheon. These books combined historical events with philosophical, religious, and social aspects, concentrating upon the dilemma of royal children who must choose between maintaining world order and achieving liberation. The *Mahabharata* is a very detailed account of the rise and fall of the Kuru dynasty. Its most famous part, the *Bhagavad Gita*, advises that it is not necessary to withdraw from the world to achieve true detachment, which lies in disinterested action, carried out for the act itself and not with a view to the ultimate result. In an inner battle man(kind) must choose between good and evil, having the opportunity to engage his divine aspect, and the gods assume human forms upon earth.

From 600 B.C. temples were built and various forms of worship evolved. The *Paranas*, a set of religious books, gave a summary of the gods and their descendents, providing instruction on how to serve and worship them. Brahma, Vishnu, and Shiva form the Great

Trinity, appearing as creator, preserver, and destroyer respectively. The caste system is explained in the *Dharma Shastras* (*Books of the Law*) written at about the same time.

Tantra is a pre-Vedic, mystical concept, utilizing the energy of every element of human nature. The Mother Goddess is called *tripura* because of her three forms, physical, subtle or verbal, and mental or transcendental. The human body is regarded as the temple of the Mother Goddess. Tantra is concerned with the body, regarding the individual as containing all the essential dimensions of the cosmos, and focuses on the union of male and female principles. Unlike Hinduism, in which the female associated with the male god is represented as smaller, Tantra gives the female equal importance, and the consort is presented in the yab-yum position, intertwined with the god. Tibetans in particular developed this form with its deities and rituals.

Buddha is seen in Hinduism as the ninth incarnation of Vishnu, dating from the period in which Buddhism gained great popularity, especially among the lower classes. Brahmins then formulated the idea that Vishnu had come to earth in order to preach a false religion, thus separating true believers from heretics. In another interpretation, Vishnu came to put an end to the arrogance and oppression of the Brahmins, and to purify Hinduism from the rituals that had grown out of hand.

Krishna is considered the most important incarnation of Vishnu, and is worshipped as a god in his own right. The name Krishna, meaning "the black one," appeared in the Upanishads, and later in detailed stories about the hero in the Mahabharata. The Puranas describe Krishna's life, and his exceptional strength, in colorful tales.

Vishnu had come down to earth to put an end to the tyranny of King Kamsa, who, when he heard about this, captured Krishna's future mother, Devaki, and murdered all her children upon birth. The black skin of Krishna, often represented as blue, resulted from Vishnu's having plucked two hairs from his head, one white and one black, which ended up in the wombs of Rohini and Devaki. Vishnu intervened to save first Krishna's older brother, Balarama, born from the white hair, and Krishna, from the black hair. The figure is also thought to have derived from the rural population of southern India, the dark-skinned Dravidians.

Called Sakyamuni in the Buddhist tradition or Krishna in Hinduism, he was born in 563 B.C. at Lumbini, in the western part of Nepal. It is said that the young Krishna grew up among cowherds, enchanting the *gopis*, girls who looked after the cows, with his flute playing and dancing with them in the moonlight; he is often depicted as dancing. Sometimes he is shown with four arms. All of the Hindu gods have "vehicles" to transport them quickly – these probably evolved first from birds, who were seen as messengers between man and the gods. The bird, or half-bird and half-human, Garuda, is depicted as a god in its own right, the king of the birds, as well as a vehicle. It can be male or female, and is often represented as golden or yellow, as at birth it was said to have been mistaken for fire due to its luminosity. It is an enemy of snakes, and can ward off snakebites, and all animal, vegetable, and mineral poisonings. Krishna rides on Garuda. Crows or ravens are emissaries of dark wrathful deities such as Mahakala.

Krishna attained enlightenment after six years of fasting and meditation, after this being called Buddha. He had many wives, of which Radha is the most important. Their love and her devotion to him became an allegory for the love between Krishna the god and his followers. Radha and Krishna also embody the tantric principles of the two aspects of the divine (male and female) which together form one.

The new doctrine of Buddhism taught that everyone could deliver himself from the cycle of rebirth through the means of a correct inner attitude, and has remained a part of Hinduism since that time. Worship of Buddha arose only after his death at the age of eighty at Kustingara, his relics being laid in eight stupas. Many of the laity who had revered him as a teacher visited and bowed before them, as did monks. Other Buddhist leaders were also honored with stupas, which formed centers of worship where later the laity gathered to hear the best monks preach. A model stupa, which might or might not contain a relic of the Buddha, was set up in these meeting places, and symbols such as the chakra and trident were added.

Buddhism addresses human suffering caused by disease, poverty, and old age, ending in death, and the vicissitudes of desire, lust, anger, greed, etc. Its essence is compassion toward all living creatures, but most of all toward oneself. Worship is not central; the goal is to liberate everyone in the world from suffering, resulting in a spiritual quest. The Buddha is worshipped as an exemplary human being who achieved enlightenment, and there are many Boddhisatwas, but Dharma – the Law – contains the philosophy and principles to acquire insight into human nature, teaching that perfection is attainable. In the same way that Hinduism absorbed gods, Buddhism has counterparts of Hindu deities, and in China took on the nature-oriented and contemplative aspects of Taoism.

In 261 B.C. King Ashok of the Maurya Empire in Bihar, India, conquered Kalinga, on the east coast of India, adjoining his kingdom; the annexation was brutal, and Ashok converted to Buddhism due to his feelings of remorse for all the suffering and loss of life entailed. Ashok has been described as the Constantine of Buddhism, and acted as a great missionary, erecting Rock Edicts to instruct the public, speaking against the killing of animals. These pillars were erected on public highways, showing that education was more general in India at the time of Ashok than ever before or since. His spreading of the word about Buddhism embraced parts of three continents: Western Asia, including Syria; Eastern Europe, including Macedonia and the Epirus; North Africa, including Egypt and Cyrene; and he established the Buddhist faith on the island of Ceylon.

A master builder, Ashoka was the first in India to build in stone. He made pilgrimages to the places associated with the Buddha, and was a munificent donor to the monastery at Sarnath. He built stupas, monasteries, places for study, hospitals, asylum for animals, saw to the planting of trees and digging of wells. His edifices helped the movement of Buddhism forward.

When he came to Nepal, he selected a site about two miles to the southwest of Kathmandu, then called Manju Patan, and founded a new capital called Lalita Patan. He was accompanied by his daughter, who with her husband made Nepal their home, founding Deva Patan near Pashupatinath Temple. They went into religious retirement in old age, each vowing to build a retreat for members of the Order:

Charumati did die within her own nunnery, but her husband was unable to complete the building of his monastery.

The Newari people are thought to be the original inhabitants of the Kathmandu Valley in the early third or fourth century A.D.; according to popular legend, the valley was a giant lake until the Bodhisattva Manjushree, brandishing a holy sword, split the hills that surround the valley and drained the giant lake, allowing Newars to settle the fertile land. Manjushree, who had the ability to see the nature of reality, is the embodiment of the Enlightened Mind or Discriminating Wisdom. He is considered the creator of the Kathmandu valley and founder of Nepalese culture.

In the Buddhist tradition the first manifestation of the primordial Buddha, or Adi Buddha, was in the form of a flame of fire or Clear Light – the latter meaning self-cognizant wakefulness present in the mind stream of all sentient beings of the three realms. Since it is present in all human beings it is called Buddha-nature of Adi Buddha. It originated at Swayambhu in Kathmandu, already a famous pilgrimage site by the fifth century A.D.

An incredibly diverse and complex system of beliefs exists in Nepal, located between India and Tibet, through the fusion of Hinduism, Tibetan Buddhism, and Tantric traditions. According to tradition, Manjushree was a Chinese Boddhisatwa who had learned by intuition of a blue flame on a lotus in the big lake of Nepal; he traveled there to offer worship, but could not reach it because of the water. With his sword he cut the southern wall of the basin and the water drained out, leaving the Kathmandu valley.

Although the vast majority in Nepal are Hindu, many are Buddhists. Lumbini, the place where Lord Buddha, the enlightened one, was born is in the Terai region of Nepal, and has long been a holy site for Buddhists all over the world. Newari people practice and study Vajrayana Buddhism in Sanskrit, and are also well known for having an incredible number of religious festivals during the course of the year, many tied to Hindu holidays, the birth of Buddha and the harvest cycle.

At Swayambhunath there is also a temple dedicated to the goddess Harati; as Buddhists had no deity in their own pantheon to protect against the dreaded smallpox, they adopted the Hindu deity for assistance. Harati was once an ogress who kidnapped other people's children every day in order to feed her 500 children. The people begged Buddha for help, and he took away the youngest child of the ogress and hid him beneath his begging bowl. After searching the world for him, Harati was compelled to go to Buddha's doorstep, whereupon Buddha returned her child. However, Harati and her children within the week found themselves starving to death. She asked for a solution from Buddha, who turned her mind to compassion, and she became non-violent. Buddha placed Harati at the head of his entire circle. She is also known as Ajima, great-grandmother of the world and a protector of all children. A child who is ill may be taken to her shrine to pray for recovery. She is also the Goddess of smallpox and other epidemics.

The visitor will find within Mahabuddha Temple in Pathan a shrine to the Hindu god Vishnu, and at Machhindranath Temple in Bungamati, Buddha has a niche in a recess surrounded by butter lamps.

Symbols also intermingle, with the eight auspicious signs in Tibetan Buddhism being the conch, the lotus, two fish, a white parasol, a banner, an endless knot, a vase, and a wheel. The conch symbolizes the blessedness of turning to the right and proclaims the glory of the gods through its humming sound. The lotus is a symbol of purity, rising white from mud, representing eternal renewal, rising above the bonds of cyclic existence, while being uncontaminated by the confusion of the world. Thus it symbolizes the possibility of enlightenment even in difficult circumstances. It is a water plant, and water creates life. The two fish signify being rescued from the ocean of misery that is earthly existence. The white parasol protects one from evil desires. The banner symbolizes the victory of Buddhism. The endless knot is a mystical diagram that stands for the endless cycle of rebirth. The wheel or *chakra* symbolizes the Wheel of the Law, which turns twelve times on three revolutions for each four Noble Truths. The eight spokes represent the Eightfold Paths. A Dharmachakra represents completion and salvation achieved through the Buddha's teachings. Newari Buddhists substitute the fly-whisk, made of yak tail attached to a silver staff, for the wheel; it symbolizes Tantric manifestations. The vase, or *kalasa*, is the treasury of spiritual wealth, and also holds water, the elixir of immortality.

An oil lamp or *sekunda*, used in Hindu rituals in Nepal, has a main part in the shape of a *kalash*, with a triangular front part inscribed with the image of Ganesh, as bestower of success and first to be worshipped in every puja. On the handle snakes, which are worshipped in the Kathmandu Valley, are engraved. *Nagas*, or serpent beings in lakes, ponds, and rivers, belong to the animal realm though they appear in the form of snakes, half snakes, and half humans with elaborate jeweled crowns. Infinitely wealthy, they owe their present form to a previous life of unethical generosity. Viewed as semi-divine, semi-demonic, patrons of waterways, lakes, and springs that guard all the treasures of the earth, they are therefore a symbol of life and fertility. Since they regenerate by shedding their skin, they represent the eternal cycle of time and immortality.

These symbols have come down from Hinduism, where a bell symbolizes the mystical primary sound, the origin of creation; it is also the symbol of Indra. In depictions of the gods, a flame, *agni*, symbolizes elemental force, and the destruction that is a precondition to the creation of new life. The swastika was first identified with Vishnu, as a solar or fire symbol, and later as an auspicious mark on his breast. Buddha was also identified by this sign. Later, it came to be associated with Shiva. The clockwise swastika represented evolution; counter clockwise, the winter sun, implying movement, time and life. In both the Hindu and Buddhist traditions, it came to symbolize the law; as a Buddhist symbol, the esoteric doctrine of Buddha.

Many ritual implements also occur as hand-held attributes of deities, and have their origins in the wrathful arena of the battlefield and the funerary realm of the cremation grounds. These are primal images of destruction, slaughter, sacrifice, and necromancy wrested from the hands of evil and used as symbols against the ultimate root of evil, ego. The wrathful deities are actually protectors, guarding from evil spirits while adjuring strict observance of religious rules. They are depicted surrounded by flames or wind, and may wear garlands of skulls or freshly severed heads; they may be stepping on corpses or writhing, dying bodies. In the hands of protective deities, weapons became pure symbols, weapons of transformation representing good rather than evil, and express the stern compassion to mercilessly destroy the manifold illusions of the inflated human ego.

A Vajrakila or Phurpa originated as a stake by which domestic animals or those intended for sacrifice were tethered; also, the position of a Vedic altar was determined by tossing a peg to the east until it remained upright in earth. The symbol is depicted as a scepter or a "magic dart" for the ritual slaying of a foe by effigy. It keeps diseases and evil spirits at bay by nailing them down and placing them under the power of Dharma, and combats enemies of the Law. It is a symbol of power, or spike, of Indra, used as a weapon to cut through hatred and stab demonic obstructions.

The sword is a symbol of wisdom and enlightenment, which may be represented by flames or luminous rays issuing from it, as well as a weapon or force of destruction used to destroy ignorance. A battle axe is the weapon of Parasuram, the sixth incarnation of Vishnu, and symbolizes the conquering of darkness and ignorance. It liberates those on a spiritual path from worldly ties.

The skull cup (*kapala* in Sanskrit) is made from the oval upper section of a human cranium, and serves as a libation vessel for a vast number of Vajrayana deities, mostly wrathful. The selection of the correct skull is of immense importance; the skull of a murder or execution victim is believed to possess the greatest Tantric power; the skull of one who died from a violent or accidental death, or virulent illness, possesses medium range magical power; the skull of a person who died peacefully in old age has virtually no occult power. The skull of a child who died during the onset of puberty has great potency, as do the skulls of miscegenate or misbegotten children of unknown paternity, born from the forbidden union of castes, out of wedlock, from sexual misdemeanor, or from incest; the "misbegotten skull" of a seven or eight-year-old child born from an incestuous union is considered to possess the greatest power in certain Tantric rituals. The vital force or potential of the skull's "previous owner" remains within it as a spirit, rendering it effective.

The skull cup may be held at the level of the heart of wrathful protective deities, and paired with a curved knife or chopper held above it. The chopper severs the life veins and vital organs of demonic enemies. Blood and organs are collected in the cup as an oblation vessel for the deity's sustenance. Such contents may include warm human blood, blood and brains, blood and intestines, human flesh and fat, the heart or the heart and lungs of an enemy, the heart of Mara or the blood of Rudra. Frequently the cups are filled with the sense organs of the human body, creating a visceral response that reiterates the impermanence of the body and urges the viewer to resist dependence on physical sensations and desires. Skull cups may be used for holding holy water; during Tibetan liturgy, a Lama might dip fingers into the bowl and flip water into the air for spirits.

A mace or club is an artifact made from human bone and has a skull at the top, giving protection to the one who carries it. It stands for the power of natural laws and of time, which destroys everything. A *kangling* is a musical instrument like a trumpet made from a human thigh-bone; it is a ritual object in Tantric worship, blown to drive away evil spirits. A scepter or *khartwanga* is made of a human bone of the forearm or leg, or sometimes of wood and metal, held by Tantric deities. It holds skulls, and may be topped with a *vajra, kapala*, trident or banner.

Mahakala, worshipped by both Hindus and Buddhists, is the protector of the doctrine of Sakyamuni, overcomer of all obstacles on the way to enlightenment. He is regarded as a manifestation of Avalokitshwara, who created him as a protector of wisdom, giving him the strength of Yama, lord of death. Mahakala has a retinue of spirits and ghosts under his command. His body is dark blue and he looks wrathful, wearing serpents as ornaments. He has a garland of severed heads and a crown of five skulls representing the five defilements (lust, hatred, delusion, pride, and jealousy).

There is a story about the Mahakala "protector chapel" at Samye monastery in Central Tibet, traditionally kept locked for most of the year with entry into its precinct rarely permitted. The attendant monk supervising the chapel annually would ceremoniously replace an iron chopper and wooden chopping board which had become blunt and worn down by its nocturnal activities; even though the chapel was locked and empty, at night the screams of ethereal miscreants hacked by Mahakala's chopper could be clearly heard from outside.

Vajrapani is the spiritual son of Akshobya, the progenitor of the Vajra family, and usually holds a *vajra* and a noose. He is blue in color, and represents the transmutation of hatred into power or energy. When the snakes came to listen to Buddha's teachings, Vajrapani was charged with protecting them from the attacks of Garudas, and to deceive them assumed a form like theirs; as the protector of snakes, he is also seen as a god of rain.

When Manjushree drained the lake from the Kathmandu valley, it is believed that creatures that dwelt there disappeared from the earth, among them Garuda; white lions, sculptures of which are found before temples and shrines; the serpent kings; *hitimangas/makars* or mythical water dragons, often depicted on water spouts and on a toran above entrance doors to temples; and Chhepu, most powerful of the aquatic animals, marked with the symbol of the moon on his forehead because it was thought he could fly to the moon.

Chhepu had two brothers, Garuda and Hitimanga; his mother had desired to give birth to a son who would be the bravest, most truthful, and endowed with marks of superiority, but becoming impatient, looked into the nest to check on his evolvement, finding him in a premature condition with only the head formed. Thus he is depicted as only a head and small hands holding snakes that he is devouring. It is also said that Chhepu disappeared from the world because he did not wish to see evil triumphant over good, as it would when Kalki came. Kalki, the last incarnation of Vishnu, has not yet appeared on earth; at the end of the present age of Kali, it is said that the earth will be shrouded in darkness, moral values will have disappeared, there will be general confusion and chaos. Vishnu will return as Kalki, shining like a comet in the sky, to save mankind by restoring Dharma, the law of justice, so that a new era of purity and peace may begin, whereupon Kalki will return to heaven.

Beliefs Regarding Death

Virtuous or non-virtuous actions performed during a lifetime create karma, which determines rebirth in any of six realms of cyclic existence. Evil deeds cause one to suffer after death and be reborn in the animal, hungry ghost, and hell-beings' realms. There are also creatures dwelling in places on earth, called landowners or guardian deities, which belong to the realm of demigods or ghosts. Not all ghosts are miserable; some are wealthy and powerful, and may appear to people as ghosts, demons, or in dreams in an infinite variety of forms, including the human. Depending on their disposition, they may help or harm.

According to *The Tibetan Book of the Dead*, the spirit of the departed goes through a process lasting forty-nine days following death. The first half-day to four days is the period of time necessary for the departed to realize that they have left their body. In the second stage the departed encounters hallucinations resulting from karma created during life, then various peaceful and wrathful deities that are actually personifications of human feelings. In order to successfully achieve nirvana, the deceased must exhibit loss of ego and not flinch from them. The final stage is the process of reincarnation.

Mandalas

For Hindus, a mandala is a circle that has universal mystical significance, a symbolic diagram invested with the spirit of a deity, who resides at the center. Finished, it is a yantra, an object of worship and a meditative device for concentration, a vehicle of empowerment. It is created by and becomes a focusing of energies. The purpose of Tantric art is the attainment of a higher level of perception; it is a visual aid for self-enlightenment.

The dot at the center is a seed, dedicated to a particular deity. From this a line materializes, and other lines form triangular geometric patterns, including the upright triangle for the masculine and inverted triangle for the female principles. The circumference represents the dynamic consciousness of the viewer; it also has a protective significance. The square represents the physical world bound in four directions, and lotus petals surrounding the circle denote regenerative power and principles. Most often the mandala represents Mt. Meru, the mythical mountain, but could also represent a city, a palace or an island. In Tantric Buddhism the mandala represents the Palace of Purity, free of obstacles and impurities. The lotus-encircled square stands for the Sacred Palace, surrounded by a circle of flames, four thunderbolts, and eight cemeteries which originally represented various funeral rites of the different Hindu castes. Mythologically, when the demon Rudra was slain, his dismembered body fell in the four cardinal and intercardinal directions, from which eight great trees grew, and are still represented, along with regional protectors, mahasiddhas, stupas, clouds, mountains, lakes, spirits, and animals, as well as corpses.

A mandala could also represent the human body – in any case, it is a powerhouse of energy. A yantra is a consecrated mandala. The best, or special, mandalas are prepared by an enlightened teacher for a disciple, not sold or bartered, but given.

For Buddhists, a mandala is primarily a symbolic mansion or citadel for the gods, from which the deity descends when invoked by the adept of the officiant. It may be made of fine, colored sand and is usually destroyed after it has served its purpose. From the original Sanskrit meaning of "circle," it implies both a basic geometric design as well as a circle of people who have come together for a common concern. The Wheel of Time, *kalachakra*, stemming from Tantric Buddhism, has become the most important one to be constructed in exile. Revolving around the concept of time and cycles – from the cycles of the planets, to the cycles of human breathing – it is meant to facilitate working with the most subtle energies within one's body on the path to enlightenment.

Continuing Emigration

"Here in New Mexico our history is a unique blend of Native, Mexican, and US national identities," says Julianna Kirwin, whose childhood in the Midwest was rich in music and art, since she had two musicians as parents. She was also very aware of her father being first generation Polish American; he used his love of music to spark the imagination of students across the state of Nebraska, engaging them in learning a stringed instrument.

When Juliana passed through New Mexico at the age of twelve, she decided she wanted to become an artist; in 1985 she bought the Silver Dollar Saloon on the main street of Bernalillo with its casita in back, and has been working out of it and fixing it up ever since. Serigraphs reflect her love of New Mexico, and monotypes present its mythology. She teaches art to K-2 students for the Bernalillo Public Schools, which is 45% Hispanic and 42% Native American, with six or seven pueblos within the school district. Blue corn thrives in her courtyard, a head start on a project on Indian Corn of the Americas that will combine principles of healthy living with art, literacy, and history. She familiarizes students with Georgia O'Keeffe in sketching and painting the landscape; celebrates the Day of the Dead complete with making piñatas and sugar skulls; and has her students make stacks of tiny adobe bricks from which they build houses, churches, and then plazas. She has achieved an alignment between work, study, artistic expression, and her love of both Mexico and New Mexico.

Julianna also belongs to a Tibetan Buddhist *sangha* in Corrales, and with students created thirteen papier-mâché masks of Tibetan deities for a performance of the *Tibetan Book of the Dead* at the VSA Theatre in Albuquerque. The masks were constructed from recycled objects, using egg cartons and even pieces of pressed tin sheeting from her building. She can transcend cultures, dipping into them as individually desired.

Masks from the Tibetan *Book of the Dead* by Julianna Kirwin.

Coming Full Circle

In the tradition of the Statue of Liberty, people still come to America, the word for which in Chinese, *mei-guo*, translates as 'the beautiful land', to live in a place where they can develop their potential. The spiritual is all encompassing. Prayer flags, wood-block printed with text or images, bless the surrounding countryside; the three flaming jewels traditionally on the back of the powerful horse in the center symbolize the Buddha, the Dharma (Buddhist teachings), and the Sangha (Buddhist community), the three cornerstones of Tibetan philosophical tradition. The colors of prayer flags correspond to the colors of the Five Buddhas, which represent water, earth, fire, wind, and space. Once hung high in the Himalayas so that the prayers would be wafted far, bringing peace for the entire world, they now hang over the landscape of New Mexico.

Like the Indians, Tibetans lived in their vast, sparsely populated country in perfect harmony with the environment, due not only to a small population and plentiful resources, but the result of an attitude of respect for all living creatures. From the time of the seventeenth century Fifth Dalai Lama, the Dalai Lamas and regents promulgated decrees for the protection of animal life and the environment, issued every year in their names, which not only forbade the killing of wild animals but also of domestic animals on certain days, such as the 8th, 15th, and 30th days of each month. These traditions continue in Tibet and in Nepal, where many Tibetan refugees went (there is a sizeable Nepali population in Albuquerque and Santa Fe now as well).

And we can think of this migration as having come full circle, from the sand paintings of the Native American to those of Tibetans, all forming a part of the Land of Enchantment. Like the *kalachakra*, there is no set beginning and no end to the saga.

Bibliography

Books and Articles

Annual Report of the Bureau of American Ethnology: vol. 9, 1887-88, p. 582; vol. 45, 1927-28, pp. 183, 290; vol. 46, 1928-29, pp 493-494; vol. 47, 1929-30, p. 632.

Chilton, Lance, Katherine Chilton, Polly Arango, James Dudley, Nancy Neary, and Patricia Stelzner. *New Mexico: a new guide to the colorful state*. Albuquerque, New Mexico: UNM Press, 1984.

Demarco, Marisa. "The King and Queen of Hopping Seeds," *Alibi*, September 27-October 3, 2007.

Garcez, Antonio R. *Adobe Angels: The Ghosts of Albuquerque*. Santa Fe, New Mexico: Red Rabbit Press, 1994.

Garcez, Antonio R. *American Indian Ghost Stories of the Southwest*. Truth or Consequences: Red Rabbit Press, 2000.

Handbook of North American Indians, vol. 9, 10.

Harris, Linda G. *Ghost Towns Alive: Trips to New Mexico's Past*. Albuquerque, New Mexico: University of New Mexico Press, 2003.

Kutz, Jack. *Mysteries & Miracles of New Mexico*. Corrales, New Mexico: Rhombus Publishing Co., 1988.

Larese, Steve and Bert Herrman. Various articles in *New Mexico Magazine*, May 2006.

National Park Service materials.

Polston, Cody. *Haunted New Mexico: The Ghosts of Albuquerque*. Baltimore, Maryland: PublishAmerica, 2004.

Salinas Pueblo Missions. Tucson, Arizona: Southwest Parks and Monuments Association, 1993.

Schlegel, Zak. "Deathly Drama," *Alibi*, October 25-31, 2007.

Varney, Philip. *NM's Best Ghost Towns*.

Weigle, Martha. *The Penitentes of the Southwest*. Santa Fe, New Mexico: Ancient City Press, 1970.

Online Sources

Wikipedia

http://www.bgsu.edu/

www.sgha.net (Southwest Ghost Hunters)

www.hanksville.org

www.lallorona.com

http://southwest.library.arizona.edu/spmc/body.1_div.34.html

http://aspiritwalker.com/PrayerSticks.htm

Klaus Trenary, Recreational Drugs Information (www.a1b2c3.com/drugs), Copyright ©: 1999-2007

www.peyote51.com

At Home Away from Home: Tibertan Culture in Exile, curated by former Curator of Asian & Middle Eastern Collections, Frank J. Korom, Ph.D., http://www.internationalfolkart.org/exhibitions/past/hah_tibet/index.html

Master of Ancient Discipline Retains Youthful Vigor, Maria Army, *The Albuquerque Journal*, June 1, 1986

The Tibetan Buddhist view of the Environment by Kim Yeshi, www.tibet.com, site maintained and updated by The Office of Tibet, the official agency of His Holiness the Dalai Lama in London.

Near-Death Experiences & the Afterlife, Kevin Williams, March 14, 2006, www.near-death.com

Nitin Kumar, Editor http://www.exoticindia.com

The Huntington Archive of Buddhist and Related Art (http://kaladarshan.arts.ohio-state.edu/), College of the Arts, The Ohio State University, Columbus, Ohio

www.archdiocesesantafe.org

chancellor@archdiocesesantafe.org